D0031685

Wabi Sabi
Timeless Wisdom for a Stress-Free Life

Wabi Sabi

Timeless Wisdom for a Stress-Free Life

Agneta Nyholm Winqvist

Translated from Swedish by
Stine Skarpnes Osttveit

Skyhorse Publishing

Skyhorse Publishing books may be purchased in bulk at special discounts for sales promotion, corporate gifts, fund-raising, or educational purposes. Special editions can also be created to specifications. For details, contact the Special Sales Department, Skyhorse Publishing, 307 West 36th Street, 11th Floor, New York, NY 10018 or info@skyhorsepublishing.com.

Skyhorse® and Skyhorse Publishing® are registered trademarks of Skyhorse Publishing, Inc.®, a Delaware corporation.

Visit our website at www.skyhorsepublishing.com.

10 9 8 7 6 5 4 3 2 1

Library of Congress Cataloging-in-Publication Data is available on file.

ISBN: 978-1-61608-881-1   5038 2133 12/12

Printed in China

Table of Contents

Foreword

When I was first asked to write a book about wabi sabi, my immediate thought was: How will I be able to put something so beautiful into words?

But just as soon as the thought hit me, I remembered that wabi sabi never demands anything of us; it is the most gentle teaching there is. I therefore wanted to make an attempt to present this deep wisdom that is just waiting to be discovered more thoroughly.

Wabi sabi is sometimes called *the religion of beauty*. "Timeless wisdom" and "humble beauty" are a few of the terms that circle this teaching. Wabi sabi gives us the wisdom to create a warm, beautiful, and rich life. A life where we do not resist, don't stress, and don't hunt after a diffuse happiness, which lies in front of so many of us as a mirage. Wabi sabi removes this illusion and gives us the insight that happiness is a fleeting feeling. If we let go of the hunt for it and instead search for gentle enjoyment in life, we will feel so much better.

Wabi sabi is seen as the heart of Japanese culture and has its roots in the Zen philosophy. The quiet Japanese Zen existence is a way of life that most of us will never even get close to today, even if we wanted to. I have therefore consciously chosen to use today's time and its possibilities and challenges as a basis in this book.

I will describe my journey in the topic and my trials in trying to change my existence and move towards a more modest and humble life. I do not always succeed, but when I meet challenges,

I remind myself of wabi sabi's basic idea: "Nothing is perfect." With that insight, I can enjoy even my own failures and my life's imperfections.

Wabi sabi has taught me to accept things as they are. I do not have to fight life at all times—I can rest, follow the flow, and let life's own power and my longing steer me instead of fighting it. Wabi sabi has also taught me to accept change, since it is unavoidable in our existence. To live with wabi sabi means maturing as a human being and learning to see our existence with sober eyes. My hope is to be able to pass this wisdom on to others.

I would like to thank the people that have inspired me—among them are Richard R. Powell, Andrew Juniper, Candice O'Denver, Joyce Rupp, Gary Thorp, Gregg Krech, and John Lane.

Wabi Sabi—The naked beauty of life

Wherever we turn in this world, we find that humans have relied on principles that contain terms like performance, determination, dedication, and development. In many ways this seemed inevitable, and yet, it seems more important than ever to find ways to live in unison with nature and ourselves. If not, there is actually a risk that we will go under.

It is daunting to think that in 1900 and 1950 a similar "development" in our part of the world took place, a development that had previously taken 6,000 years. Between 1950 and 1970, there was another revolution of the same size, and it has since then continued like this, at an accelerating pace. Today, we might learn as much in a month as we would over 6,000 years, and in a year maybe we can learn as much in a day as we would over 6,000 years . . . Is it then surprising that many in today's society feel confused, tired, and shaken?

Wabi Sabi speaks of something completely different. Wabi sabi is something we can all find in silence, quiet, and thought; the wisdom is similar to mindfulness and simple living—a teaching that has quickly spread during the past few years in the Western world.

Wabi sabi is the tender mother that embraces her children. She gives them nourishment, leads them, and gently points them towards a stable life. Maybe it is Gaia, the spirit of earth, that is watching over wabi sabi? I therefore chose to refer to wabi sabi in the feminine form, as a "she," because it is how I perceive the subject—like a wise, older, loving feminine spirit.

When you first get in touch with wabi sabi on a deep level, it is common to first want to rest. This is followed by a vulnerable melancholy, which sneaks up on us and makes us ask questions like, Where am I? Does what I do work? Is this the way I want my children to grow up?

The topic is timeless—it has no gurus or teacher, and it is based on the wisdom of nature. If you want to learn the truth of wabi sabi, you need to stay within these three principles and let them sink in:

- Nothing lasts forever
- Nothing is perfect
- Nothing is ever finished

Once you have incorporated these truths in your inner self, then you will find that you are close to the wabi sabi core. The spirituality of wabi sabi is beyond words. The more we try to dress spirituality in words, the further it slips away from us. Wabi sabi is the timeless wisdom about life that you cannot question. If we really want peace of mind, we have to allow this wisdom to be part of ourselves.

Wabi and sabi—the meaning of the words

Wabi sabi has its roots in the Japanese Zen philosophy. In the beginning, this teaching was used to create environments for meditation and reflection, both inside and outside in nature. The idea was to form an environment where humans could empty their minds and obtain a complete presence. As part of this, drinking tea, among other things, was an important ritual. Rituals have always had an important place in Japanese culture.

"Wabi" on its own describes a voluntary simplicity related to life; a voluntary poverty that contains life's real riches. "Wabi" stands for everything we wish for that cannot be bought with money. "Wabi" makes us embrace a different relationship with life's worries—sickness, unemployment, longing after loved ones lost. "Wabi" doesn't try to cower or shy away from the fear, sorrow, or pain. "Wabi" stares the hardships straight in the eye and learns to live with them, without allowing it to destroy life.

Initially, "wabi" was a way of arranging the environment around the tea-drinking ritual for the Japanese aristocrats during the 1500s and 1600s. "Wabi" would strip the surrounding environment to make it as simple and Spartan as possible. This was done to make the true values become clearer and stronger. It was the tea masters, Zen priests, and monks that promoted the teaching. The philosophy has had a large impact on the Japanese way of relating to literature, poetry, architecture, design, gardening, and cooking.

The word "sabi" was initially a way of describing the naked beauty in poetry (especially from the 1200s and 1300s.) It may be translated to "the times blossom"—an expression that speaks of how everything will age. "Sabi" represents the passage of time. There is a large sense of longing in the word, but also a hint of melancholy that nothing lasts forever.

When "wabi" and "sabi" were first matched together, a quality was born that we could almost translate into a "humble beauty." Wabi sabi is a counterpart to "too much," and if we place it in a historical per-spective, we can see that we have reached a point where "too much" has become too large—many eat too much, stress too much, work too much, talk on the phone too much, shop too much, exercise too much. This "too much" has made many of us sick, despairing, and indolent.

> **Key words within wabi sabi**
>
> timeless wisdom
> all-embracing, unconditional love
> humility
> stillness
> reverence
> respect
> nature's wisdom
> incomplete and imperfect
> calm in change
> timeless beauty
> nature's wisdom
> modesty
> appreciation / cooperation
> sustainable development
> life in the moment
> spirituality beyond words

The feminine power

In almost every single culture, there has been an element of worship of the female power. But we don't need to go 8,000 to 10,000 years back in time to find an age where simplicity prevailed as a lifestyle, where the natural changes and rhythms of life were praised and celebrated, and where we lived in balance with nature.

In line with "modernization" and industrialization, we have tried to hide the feminine power away for a very long time. Almost without exception, we will let the masculine power react.

The feminine and the masculine powers have different standpoints and different goals. When the masculine power observe, for instance, the woods, it may think: What can I use this wood for? When the feminine power observes the woods, it considers: How can I live in balance with the forest and both give nurture to it and receive nutrients from it?

In order to create a good and sustainable life, we need to find a balance between these two powers. Wabi sabi helps us create this balance through reverence, gratitude, and reflection.

In eastern countries, they often talk about the polarity of the feminine (yin) traits and the masculine (yang) traits. Wabi sabi is a yin-subject, while, for instance, feng shui is about the balance between yin and yang. It is important to stress that the feminine and respectively masculine in this context is not the same as woman versus man. All humans carry both yin and yang qualities within, regardless of gender, and we all need to achieve a balance between the two. However, you can say that women may have a stronger yin-power, the same way men will often contain a stronger yang-power. (This might be a reason for the fact that women often burn out and suffer from exhaustion and depression in our current society, which is dominated by a yang-power.)

The feminine principle within and behind the religions

"Wisdom" is a key word within wabi sabi. Wisdom is different from knowledge, which is usually in high esteem these days. In Greek, Latin, and Hebrew, "wisdom" is a word in feminine form. She may behave subtle and fragile, but may also show herself in full force if needed. Wisdom is the mother, the earth, nature, and life. She represents goodness, love, mercy, and compassion.

If we seek within and behind the various religions and cultures, we will find the same phenomenon—namely that once there was a feminine aspect that has since been forgotten.

In Japan, she is called *Amaterasu*; in China, *Kuanyin*; in Tibet, *Tara*; in Egypt, *Isis*; in India, *Shakti*; in Greece, *Gaia*; in Kabbalah, *Shekinah*; in Christianity, *Virgin Mary*. Even in the Muslim world there are signs of the feminine power. There, the God is called *Al Rahmin*, the merciful and compassionate, and the word "rahmin" has roots in the Arabic word for "uterus," and reminds the Muslims of God's feminine qualities.

I have chosen to refer to wabi sabi as "she," and I think we have been waiting for her for quite some time. She can create life, and she can protect life for both men and women. She is the indivisible awareness we all carry.

In the Bible's the Book of the Wisdom of Solomon, you can read the following in chapter 7, verses 17–27:

> [...] For he hath given me certain knowledge of the things that are, namely, to know how the world was made, and the operation of the elements: The beginning, ending, and midst of the times: the alterations of the turning of the sun, and the change of seasons: The circuits of years, and the positions of stars: The natures of living creatures, and the furies of wild beasts: the violence of winds, and the reasonings of men: the diversities of plants and the virtues of roots: And all such things as are either secret or manifest, them I know.

> For wisdom, which is the worker of all things, taught me: for in her is an understanding spirit holy, one only, manifold, subtil, lively, clear, undefiled, plain, not subject to hurt, loving the thing that is good quick, which cannot be letted, ready to do good, Kind to man, steadfast, sure, free from care, having all power, overseeing all things, and going through all understanding, pure, and most subtil, spirits. For wisdom is more moving than any motion: she passeth and goeth through all things by reason of her pureness. For she is the breath of the power of God, and a pure influence flowing from the glory of the Almighty: therefore

can no defiled thing fall into her. For she is the brightness of the everlasting light, the unspotted mirror of the power of God, and the image of his goodness. And being but one, she can do all things: and remaining in herself, she maketh all things new: and in all ages entering into holy souls, she maketh them friends of God, and prophets [...]

Haikumoments

No happiness lasts forever. In wabi sabi, the goal is to seek for enjoyment and something called haikumoments (haiku is also a short poem). A haikumoment is a moment where everything stands still—you are observing something, open your heart, and you are filled with reverence. When you are untrained in wabi sabi, you might be able to remember one or two single moments like these in your life. For me, one of those moments was when I saw my daughter take her first steps.

The beauty of wabi sabi is that you'll experience plenty of these moments as you train your way of observing, resting, and enjoying your surroundings. It doesn't necessarily have to be about the extravagant and spectacular events, but rather the small moments you experience every day. You allow yourself to be caught in the moment and stay for a blink of an eye, and afterwards you can quietly let it go. You can never force a haikumoment, forcefully retain the moment, or try to recreate it. It is just there waiting for us.

Inside each of us
there awaits a wonder
full
spirit of freedom

she waits
to dance
in the rooms
of our heart
that are closed
dark and cluttered

she waits
to dance
in the spaces
where negative feelings
have build barricades
and stock-piled weapons

she waits
to dance
in the corners
where we still
do not believe in our goodness

inside each of us
there awaits
a wonder
full
spirit of freedom

she will lift light feet
and make glad songs
within us
on the day we open the door of ego
and let the enemies stomp out

JOYCE RUPP, FROM THE STAR IN MY HEART

The main focus of Wabi Sabi

Embrace the following:

Be careful with the following:

Embrace the following:	Be careful with the following:
Focus on nature	Focus on technology
Authenticity	Copies
Permitting natural aging	Striving for constant youth
Subtlety	Boasting
Intuitive	Rational
Unique	Mainstream, adjusted
In the moment	In the future or the past
Whole	Detached, separate
Personal	Impersonal
Appreciative	Critical, disparaging
Paradoxical, contradictory	Black/white
Unrefined, natural	Refined, studied
Decorated	Ornamented
Fractal	Squared and specified measurements
Organic	Geometric
Alive	Artificial
Artisanal	Mass-produced
Soft	Sharp
Clear and apparent	Imagined
Reflective, attentive	Ignorant, soulless
Listening, receptive	Arrogance
Seeing	Reporting
Slow	Quick
Humility	Pride
Sincerity	Heartless

Rest

The most central term in wabi sabi is rest and afterthought. Resting is so much more than what we in the Western world have made it out to be. We often think of rest as the bed, the couch, the weekend, and holidays. But according to wabi sabi, resting is to be in contact with our conscience, our wisdom, relaxing, and breathing.

We should not be in conflict with the occurrences of life—we should observe, rest, and let things take their course.

We humans often want to steer our lives in a certain direction, but life has a direction of its own that we may follow through relaxing and floating with it. Of course we may steer towards certain goals and wish for things along the way, but life will always have its set road—a road that is not always easy and without sorrow, but that leads to a good destination. We will experience much loss along the way, of that we can be certain. But the ability to feel sorrow over someone or something is evidence of our ability to love. Sorrow is the price of love.

To rest means lowering your shoulders and surrendering to the occurrences of life, but it is not the same as giving up. We are so afraid of sorrow, anger, fear, and melancholy, but it is not until we accept these as worthy friends of life that we can reach the satisfaction and peace of mind that wabi sabi stands for.

Someone wise once said, "If life was as easy as we wanted it to be, we would most likely die of boredom." This is most likely true. Whether we are religious or not, we need to take a look at our utopian fantasies at times and observe life as it is. Sometimes it is not beautiful—it can be hard to find the charm when our backs are hurting or we failed at work. But these things are a part of life, and if we can rest in it, we heal, and life gets a deeper meaning. And it is in this depth that the beauty is created.

To rest while conscious is to rest in oneself and the creative power that controls the universe—the power that makes us wake up every morning and move on with our lives without effort. Most of the body will function without any effort on our part. I view this as a divine intelligence and a creating power larger than life itself.

We are not meant to be able to see the road ahead—instead, we have to walk with the knowledge that our feet know where to go. When we exercise resting while conscious, we will walk the road through life with as little resistance as possible. We are not fighting life, but rather we accept what we cannot change and try to find the courage to change the things we can. If we cannot work up the courage we need, we will have to be at rest with that as well. We simply stop resisting, against life and against ourselves. The consciousness we are resting in will show us the right way.

Many confuse rest with being passive and sitting still. But resting can be very dynamic. We can rest while lifting weights or in the middle of a conflict—what happens while we rest is that we fully know what is going on, and we connect with the situation and ourselves.

When I am placed in situations where I feel insecure and do not see an escape, I try to find rest in consciousness. In this state I can hopefully see my own role and see where I am—see the reason for the occurrence, how it can be solved, and what the most gentle and loving road to the solution will be. This process can be a painful experience that can strike right through my body, and yet, I know I have to let it be.

The first time I fully embraced the term "rest in consciousness" and understood the meaning of it was when the following happened:

During this time I had a person in my life that would often bring out the worst sides of me; a person who never understood what I was saying. He had annoyed me for years; he was without boundaries and socially handicapped. One day he called, and after our conversation, I felt that I just couldn't deal with the situation anymore. At that point I heard my inner self say "rest in this!" I lowered my shoulders and focused on resting. For about 30 seconds my body was rebelling—it was turning and twisting and I moaned loudly. Then, it was over. It took me less than a minute to reach peace of mind, and it was through only focusing and relaxing.

This is an example of what happens if we allow ourselves to really rest. The body knows how to handle these kinds of situations all on its own, and sometimes it will be through sound and motion.

Another thing I discovered in this moment was when exactly this man had gotten to me emotionally. Now I have resolved this within myself, and no matter what this person says to me today, I can rest in my calmness and even feel a tenderness towards his hardships in life. I now take him for who he is and not for what I think he should be. In short, I have given up on my thoughts and opinions about him.

To be able to be at piece with everything that happens is life's naked beauty.

To rest through the pain

As long as we are unable to rest in pain and accept it, it will eat us up inside—it will stagnate inside of us and steal our energy.

I have gotten my portion of pain in life. Before I could accept this as a fact and stop fighting it, the pain and bitterness had made my back askew.

A while back I lost something that I had been desperately afraid of losing. When it happened something very surprising happened: I fell into an emptiness without boundaries (I have always been very afraid of the emptiness), but out of this emptiness rose a deep silence and acceptance. Neither fear nor sorrow arose in me, which was what I was certain would happen—rather, I experienced wonder and a bit of melancholy.

I lost something; a situation I had hoped would never happen did, and I had no idea where the road would lead me. But at the same time I could feel that it was leading somewhere. In the silence I could only hear the weak tones of the longing that once were. Even if the melancholy and sorrow sometimes grab me, everything still feels beautiful. There is a fragile beauty in life, and all of its occurrences are hurtful as well as enjoyable.

A young woman once wrote on Facebook: "I do not understand why happiness and sorrow always have to go hand in hand." When I really thought about this statement, I fully realized the weight of knowing that sorrow is the price of love.

The depth of our sorrow is a guide to how much we can love. The sorrow has to be there, because imagine if the opposite should be true: That we should never fear the loss of what we love?

The fear gives us something. It challenges us by reminding us that nothing lasts forever. Take care of your moment right now; give love to the person next to you. Give your partner, your child, or your friend the little extra attention that shows them that you see him or her. We should never take each other for granted, for we never know when we will be forced apart. Everything has an ending, but the beauty is that everything also has a new beginning, continually. It is never too late to start over. It is never too late to start showing your love.

Resting through pain, sorrow, and despair is so freeing that it creates a space within us where we are allowed to live in the moment. Everything doesn't need to be fixed or arranged, cleaned or put away. Let it be as is, give it the time it needs, let it hurt as much as it wants. Because in the rest there is also the knowledge that everything passes.

Let it pass

The eastern philosophy's core holds the thought that we should let things and occurrences pass. Imagine a life where everything that happens is allowed to pass on in the gentle flow of life. Where nothing unhealthy nests in your head or creates obstacles along the way. Where nothing is worth getting annoyed or worried. Where you just absorb what happens. Doesn't that sound wonderful?

Obviously, this doesn't mean that we shouldn't speak up if something feels wrong! But it is my belief that most of what we spend time worrying and fussing about is completely unnecessary. Life will never be perfect—that is wabi sabi's most important message to us.

There is a side of us that looks out for wrongs and failures, and this is a survival strategy that we need. Without it, we might end up in a bad situation, but this side controls our thoughts and judgment too often. In the rest there is no evaluation—things just are.

Every 24 hours, 50,000 to 60,000 thoughts buzz through our heads. Most of them are recurring, as we reinforce our thoughts all the time. Wabi sabi allows us to accept this flow and just thoughts pass on. The thoughts are not the problem in itself; it is when we capture them and start painting them over and over that we run into problems.

To rest means observing our thoughts as clouds in the sky that come and go. Sometimes it rains and sometimes the sun is shining, but it doesn't matter as long as we are able to be at rest in our conscious state.

We can absorb knowledge and wise thoughts, but wisdom can only be obtained through deep rest and reflection. The wisdom we then obtain may not contain what we wanted it to, but in our hearts we can feel that it is right. Wisdom never speaks with a loud voice and never requests more than we can handle. It should never say things like quit your job, change your partner, move abroad, or deconstruct your life and start over. It should whisper words that give you courage and strength to take the steps you have to take without struggle or battle.

That doesn't mean that the voice cannot awake fear and vulnerability in us—but the message is always gentle.

One of my closest friends has lost two children. When I see how life has shaped her to tenderness and humility, I realize that we so often scream after so much, while all of life's riches are lying right by our feet. It is only silence that allows us to see this. My friend who lost two boys has been able to support other people though their sorrows and losses. She rose up in her sorrow, followed life, and gave her intelligent insights as a gift to others. That jump, the healing beauty, and the silence that she shares is invaluable to others who have lost someone they loved.

There have been times when I have been intensely in love in life, times when I have danced wildly and inhibited, and there are still times where I have a great appetite for life. But the greatest passion is when life deepens. This opens the road of piety, which is calmer, deeper, and real.

Passion can be as tiring as it is intense; it is part of life, just like sorrow and happiness. I do not underestimate its value, but I think it is just as dangerous to rely too much on passion—just like it is dangerous to rely on happiness and euphoria. But if we allow passion to arise from the deep rest and devotion to life, it will not steal our from our energy. We should let it gently open doors inside of us, instead of us tearing the doors open by force. When we move slowly, with resting steps, we move forward faster, according to wabi sabi. It is when we stop trying to change things and let ourselves be at rest with them that they show us the right path.

Who looks outside, dreams; that looks inside, awakes.

C.G. JUNG

Tenderness

> I stopped searching for the truth and searched for tenderness.
>
> MARCEL PROUST

In our search for truth, we are often quite hard on ourselves, the people around us, and last but not least, our common planet. We struggle for our truths and fight for them. The longing to be "right" is often so strong that we lose track of what happens in the wake of our own justice and our need to understand issues.

This is where tenderness is important. It is a rare gift that doesn't make much of itself. It lives in the silent and modest, and it is partly lost and hidden in our community. The tenderness is in many ways a choice. To reach it, we have to be prepared to redirect our focus.

I went for a walk a while back and thought about how much tenderness I personally felt in need of. I also thought of how sad it is that tenderness has such a small place in our community. There is much talk of ethics, morals, and empathy—but nobody can heal wounds like tenderness can. Life gives us many occasions to exercise tenderness—for on my walk that day, a man suddenly stood in front of me, about to jump off the train bridge we were both on.

There are certain moments where everything goes quiet; moments when everything freezes to ice and you stand numb. When my mind awakened again, I slowly approached him. I stood next to him and awkwardly touched his arm. He looked at me mournfully. I could see that drugs and a hard life had ravaged him. I had no idea what to do, and the only thing that escaped my mouth was a few careful words in an attempt to keep him from going forth with his plan.

I tried to act like I had practiced—to rest in the situation, give in, and let the wisdom find the best solution. The answer came quickly, and I was not at all prepared for how it looked. As if from nowhere, another man came riding by on a bicycle, almost as intoxicated as the man on the bridge. He didn't acknowledge me, but rather he started shouting at the man without restraint, he said that he was a coward and would never dare to take his own life. Then he said the tenderest words I could ever imagine in such a situation: "Jump on the back, and we'll go home and eat some food and have a few beers . . ."

Tenderness is to always see the best in other people and open one's heart without prejudice, no matter the situation. I couldn't help but smile when they both rode away on the bike.

Are we sufficiently tender on our journey through life? I have had trouble with this, but I know that if I am not tender, it will tear me apart. I will often ask myself the following question: "What is the most loving thing I can do right now?" A tender voice then rises from inside of me that always knows what is best to do.

Life is tender in itself. It is when we squabble with life that the pain arises—when we want things to be different from what they are, and we get stuck with an inability to move on.

Reconciliation and forgiveness

Many years ago, I worked with a group of unemployed teens in a project about personal growth. One of the guys in the group never really spoke. He looked like a classic hip-hopper, with jeans that hung low on his hips, caps that hid half his face, a jerky walk, and a skateboard under his arm. At one point we talked about what was needed to create good relationships. Suddenly this young man opened his mouth and said: "The most important is the Jesus principle." On my questioning this, he answered that it meant that one has to learn to forgive and reconcile with what happens. Then he explained what would happen if one didn't, and he did it in a way that we couldn't misunderstand.

"If you do not reconcile with what happens, you walk around with loads of chairs and a table around your neck. You move forward slowly, you hurt all the time, and you struggle so much with the chairs and tables that you fail to see everything else happening around you."

I remember feeling completely caught off guard. Personally I felt full of the injustice I had experienced and of hidden bitterness, and part of me wanted to scream: "There are certain things that cannot be forgiven. . ."

But this guy saw right through me with a steady stare. Then he lowered his voice and said, as if he had heard my thoughts: "The choice is yours—the result is yours." In that moment I understood that this guy knew what he was talking about, and that he was right. He had freed himself, and the gift he gave us was indispensible. I was forced to start looking closer at my explanations and excuses for holding on to things and see the consequences of my choices.

It can be easy to see the power of reconciliation, but it can be extremely hard to fathom the idea when you are standing there hurt and disappointed. But everything has its time. Let things evolve and heal on its own, do not force the process. Rest in each step and life will carry you in the right direction.

Life is what it is

In three words I can sum up everything I've learned about life:
It goes on.

ROBERT FROST

On the day that I am writing this, it is one year since my father died. A silent sadness grows in my heart. I missed him for 35 years, I hated him for 15, loved him for five—and today I have mourned him for one year . . .

There are few people who are allowed to walk through life without stumbling on stones and injuring themselves. My father disappeared out of my life when I was 5, and I met him again as an adult when I was 35 years old. His life was broken in many ways, and when he died of a brain hemorrhage it was the police who finally found him weeks after. He had a picture of his children in his hand when they found him. In a traditional eulogy, it would be impossible to call his life beautiful.

The gentle voice of wabi sabi that quiets sorrow whispers that life is as it is, that death and pain are not mysteries that should be resolved or fixed, that death rather lives with us in every moment. One breath dies and another is born—it is an endless circle of life. We have to do what we can with what we have, where we are—like former United States President Theodore Roosevelt once said. In this way, we silence the hunger for the perfect life; a hunger that can never give us true satisfaction.

Death and the thought of separation is the basis of much fear within us. I heard a story told by Carol Parrish-Harra, who is a "death and dying counselor" (a person who follows and supports a dying person through the entire process) at the Sophia Foundation in United States. The story was about a small wave that was afraid to reach land, because then it knew that it would end. The closer it came to land, the more scared it became. And so a larger and wiser wave sailed up next to the small wave, and it said, "When you reach land, you open up and you become part of the ocean and you are born into new waves, so give in." Life, death, and rebirth is an endless, fantastic theater.

Devotion to life is one of the cornerstones of wabi sabi. To always say yes to whatever happens, even if it is about sorrow or pain, life or death. Every "no" I utter keeps my power down, and every "yes" I breathe opens my body in devotion. The "no" and the resistance towards even just one, as well as all of the others, creates separation and distance, while the small "yes" can create a whole ocean of closeness and intimacy with all forms of life.

When I have thought of my dad and all the sorrow and despair that followed in the wake of his life, I can feel my insides shrink into a "no"—but now there is on a large "yes" within me, even when it comes to his life.

I often think about what the word content means. I even have a T-shirt that has the word CONTENT printed on it that people often react to. A man came over to me in a store and said, "How wonderful!" Another mumbled: "Are there really women that are content?" I have also been told that the T-shirt is insolent and provocative.

But what does content really mean? To me it means to not have ideas about how things should be, but rather accept things as they are and resting in whatever happens. The soul is always content; it observes the phenomenon it is to be human and does not judge what it sees. It simply states how it is to be human—sometimes we are hungry, sometimes we are angry, sometimes we hurt, and sometimes we do silly things. But that doesn't affect the soul, which is always content.

Wabi sabi takes us to the depth of contentment and modesty; she helps us to be content with "little." And when we are content with little, we see the grandeur in the little, and then we are veiled in a calm shine. I am not trying to say that I cannot enjoy abundance, but I no longer carry a need for it.

Fifteen years ago, I was going to a lecture for the governance in one of Sweden's largest municipalities. They had booked me in a hotel that was so luxurious and grand that I was boggled. The TV set was so advanced that I couldn't work it myself. And the breakfast consisted of so much food that I didn't know how to act. Yes, I would have loved to try many of the foods offered, but I was left with distaste for the whole thing. Why this abundance? I ended up choosing what I always eat for breakfast. I made an effort to enjoy the event, but it left me with a bitter aftertaste.

The spontaneous river

> When nothing is sure, everything is possible.
>
> MARGARET DRABBLE

Life is in constant movement—everything awakens, grows, ages, decays, and dies to once again awaken and start all over. I want to compare life to an infinite wave that builds, breaks, and retracts, over and over again.

We wear ourselves down when we are unwilling to accept life's rhythm, rather than embracing what grows and awakens, the youth and the sun. We have to understand that aging, the night, and the dark are just as important. Life is constantly changing. The fear, sorrow, and tears always accompany the happiness and laughter.

We are often fixed with breathing in and fear breathing out, which will come when we relax and let things take their course. Wabi sabi allows us to breathe out, lower our shoulders, and be at rest with the fact that things will turn out the way they are supposed to. We are not supposed to be in complete control of our lives. We cannot decide what's to happen in every instance, but we can trust that it will end well. We have to try to learn to follow along with an open heart and see what happens. In wabi sabi this is called *wu wei*, and it is about letting things take their course without interfering. The movement in life is born spontaneously when we follow the river. When our reason tries to control it, *wu wei* disappears.

In order to manage this masterpiece, one of the first steps to take is to stop planning and building too many notions and expectations. We can have a wish and a longing for where our lives should lead, but in the end we have to trust life itself.

It was very hard for me to stop planning my life. I was simply terrified that it would collapse. And yes, in certain instances silly things happened, but nothing dangerous came out of it. The fear is never concentrated on right now; it is always focused on a future scenario that, in most instances, doesn't happen. A wise person once said: "To worry is to pay interest on things you may never buy."

Wabi sabi will not turn your life upside-down unless it is absolutely necessary. As the good mother she is, she would never lecture or be hard on her children. Rather, she takes them by the hand and

approaches carefully, with an enormous patience. She would never criticize you for failing at something you wanted to do. She would just stand still and wait until you are ready and mature enough to continue on.

The spontaneous river in everyday life

What do your days look like? Are they so packed with activities that you have no time left to see and feel what is really happening? Are you running between meetings and meals and always on your way to the next thing? The best way to quickly break such a pattern is to radically remove birthday parties, parent meetings, planning meetings, and everything else that is not absolutely vital, and take a flow break for a while. This will give you a chance to feel what is really important.

Wabi sabi is not pretentious or demanding; it is about creating a life with the least amount of effort. As such, we have to follow the flow and spontaneity. If we exist in the future, we miss our current life. We are often "there" instead of "here," but we are living right now and this is where we should and have to be. If we are really present in the moment, the best basis for the next step and the future will be created—we should never walk ahead of events.

The further into wabi sabi we come, the clearer it becomes that everything has its time. If something is not created with ease, but rather demands great effort, then the timing is not right for it. Put simply, we could say that, "If it is right, it's light. If it is light, it is right." The reason for this is that the light or easy things work with life and its rhythm.

I have spent too much time trying too hard in my life. I have found myself at the forefront of people that beat themselves bloody for various things. At some point I realized that this was wrong, but the collective society voice said that it was only hard work that really counted for anything.

But we don't need to work so hard if we work with the rhythm of life and dare to stop and wait until we are on the right track. We should do our work, and we should do it with enthusiasm, but it should be with light feet, open eyes, and a constant enthusiasm for, and curiosity about, what may happen.

This may sound very simple just saying it, but naturally it can be a lot harder to actually practice. If you do not dare to let go of life, ask yourself: "What is the worst that can happen?" And if the worst happens: "Can I live with it?"

What we often meet when we ask these questions is the notion of what other people will think. We seem to worry more about the reactions we will receive than what we might be exposed to.

I remember the reaction I met the first time I said to a couple of parents in my daughter's class that I would not be going to the parents' meeting because I was tired. The parents' meetings are sanctified in our community, but what should be even more sanctified is showing our children how to take care of ourselves. If we are tired, we should rest; if we are hungry, we should eat; and so on. I always try to go to the parents' meetings, but we also need to learn to listen to what the moment is telling us. And at some point, maybe my daughter would gain more from a spontaneous bubble bath with her mother instead of me stressing away at a parents' meeting.

> Being spontaneous is to do a good deed without thinking about it being a good deed.
>
> A.A. MILNE, FROM WINNIE THE POOH

Our bodies won't last long if we always prioritize our duties; every "have to" and all the burdens. Start with a short while—a lunch break or an afternoon—when everything may be exactly as you wish. Walk out the door and just see where your feet lead you. . . Do not plan the weekend, do not plan the holiday; but rather see where the spontaneity of life can take you. Wabi sabi can promise that no matter what happens, and how it feels, it will be rewarding in the long run. Some things may end in tears and anxiety, but that is not a static or never-ending state; it follows the same principle as everything else in life. If you give in completely, it will be over in no time, and life will start over once more.

It is a magical experience when you start to discover how life continuously starts over. Life itself continues indefinitely—even if it changes its shape. If you can accept this, the much-wanted peace of mind soon follows.

I cannot imagine a higher goal in life than peace of mind. It is created only when we have realized that we cannot control life; that we have to let go and accept the ways of life. I often return to the prayer for peace of mind in the twelve-step program: "God, help me accept what I cannot change, give me the courage to change what I can, and the wisdom to know the difference."

Think about the flowers that stand on the meadow day after day, despite the fact that there might be no one there to see them or enjoy them—they just stand there and wait for the next phase. They are not eager to bud, nor are they sad over their decay. Their life process goes on without effort and evaluation. It would be wonderful if we could follow their way of life; we, who despite everything, are part of nature as well. Why should we live any differently?

Timeless spiritual principles

> Life is really simple, but we insist on making it complicated.
>
> CONFUCIUS

To allow wabi sabi to be our companion on our journey through life allows us to slowly but surely pick up spiritual, all-consuming principles that build and support a strong basis.

I can tell that I have always searched for the principles that wabi sabi stand for, and now when I look in my baggage, I have found that fellowship with others has been the greatest gift I could give myself. Fellowship is always somewhere for the ones who are open to it.

If I, in my work as a mentor, need to support people who are going through rough patches and need companionship, I suggest the twelve-step association This association has self-help groups that often have an amazing fellowship. The basis of twelve-step organizations such as AA (Alcoholics Anonymous) and FAA (Food Addicts Anonymous), is to acknowledge that we at times stand powerless to control what is happening, and that it might be better to give in to a larger power. How you view that power and what you call it is individual. The twelve-step program talks about self-reflection, redemption, and a will to spread a positive message. But fellowship is the basis.

I also find the tools *honesty* and *sincerity* in wabi sabi, but not honesty and sincerity at any cost. Once again I return to the question: "What is the most loving thing I can do?" Sometimes that is to simply be quiet and let things pass. The ability to reflect and nakedly search oneself is the road to the good life, a life in depth and stability. This was what the Japanese Zen masters wanted to mediate through their tea rituals, where the teaching of wabi sabi first spread.

Other spiritual principles are *compassion* and *respect*. That is all about seeing what really hides in people. When we look at a person who is acting in a way that we do not like or respect, we are able see that her actions are a result of her needs not being met. Often we can even guess what this need may be if we really try.

If your colleague comes in to the office in the morning and is both annoyed and angry you may be able to guess why. She may have slept badly, had trouble with her car, suffer from PMS, been fighting with her partner, or something else. The question is, what is the best way to approach her—to stroke her shoulder and give her a cup of coffee, or to think that she should get it together and "find her place in the chain"—this "chain" that we so often believe we know what is.

Humor is also one of our timeless spiritual tools. The ability to look at life with humor, to be able to laugh about things that come our way, and let things pass with a smile is priceless. This is a skill worth exercising and building. Some have it for free, and others have to practice.

I remember the Oscar-winning movie *Life Is Beautiful,* a romantic comedy by and with Roberto Benigni, where the Italian Jew Guido Orefice is deported to a concentration camp with his wife and young son during the Second World War. Guido makes it his mission to keep everyone's spirits up—his ability to spread joy is a gift he gives his son and the other children in the camp. The movie shows us that we cannot always choose what happens in life, but we can always choose how we handle what happens to us.

Laughter is so freeing when you look at it from a deeper perspective. If we can laugh at our failures, we have already won much.

Dignity and integrity are other catchwords in wabi sabi. This is about being stable, with both feet planted on the ground, a straight back, head held high, and an open heart. As a woman, it also means being anchored in her pelvis and her womb. You can often tell if a woman is comfortable in her body—it shows in her walk and her way of moving. There is a weight and a dignity to her; her voice is clear and calm. When a woman says "no" from this perspective, everyone know that it really means no (children are experts at this—they know if a "no" is a no or not). She renders respect and a motherly calm. To live a worthy life gives us the ability to die satisfied.

Integrity is about knowing yourself and your needs, and then satisfying them so that you have the energy to keep the flame alive. It is also about living a life where you know you have to do certain things even when it is not your choice, and to look at oneself as a serving being. To serve life is the most important skill we can learn. The one who has taken this knowledge in will no longer see him or herself as the most important being in the universe. The truth is that in other people you meet yourself—so why not serve everything and everyone as best as you can?

This does, however, demand one note: To be able to give, we cannot be empty ourselves. Therefore, we have to fill ourselves first and then share of our abundance. A beautiful metaphor is to look at your own heart: The heart beats double beats (thump-thump). During the first beat, the heart is filled with blood, and during the next beat, it gives its abundance to the rest of the body. Many people, women in particular, do the exact opposite. They first give out energy and then later try to refill themselves, if there is anything left. . . This is not enough in the long run.

It is possible to serve life without losing energy if we allow ourselves to rest in what we do. We often carry a strange notion that we should work hard and then go home and rest, work hard and then take a holiday, work hard and then sleep. . . The timeless wisdom says that, instead, we should rest in what we do. This way, we do not lose energy, and we can recognize when enough is enough.

To know when "enough is enough" is an interesting wabi sabi phenomenon. When life goes 100 miles an hour, we are unable to recognize what our bodies are saying. We don't hear when our souls are screaming, "Calm down!" We see burnout and exhaustion everywhere when people do not have the time to ask themselves the question, "Is this enough now?"

Lastly, we risk losing ourselves in something we cannot get out of. We see all kinds of habits—of games, sex, food, Facebook, and more—that we easily lose ourselves in just because we haven't learned to recognize when enough is enough.

We will in the future see more spiritual principles that support the principle of being human, and that slowly but surely will gather the religions and crystalize their best parts. If we build upon the inner and outer world with these spiritual principles as a basis, we will have the opportunity to obtain a really good life down deep. The following catchwords have great significance:

Acceptance

Responsibility

Empathy

Fantasy

Forgiveness

Reconciliation

Trust

Fellowship

Generosity

Atonement

Honorable

Hope

Humor

Insight

Integrity

Creativity

Love

Compassion

Awareness

Meaningfulness

Courage

Presence

Reliability

Respect

Gratitude

Confidence

Tolerance

Belief

Faithfulness

Patience

Willingness

Friendliness

Reverence

Honesty

Humility

Openness

Surrender

The humble road—naikan

We don't see things as they are, we see them as we are.

ANNAIS NIN

In Japanese culture, there is a disciplinary exercise called *naikan*. This is important in wabi sabi. There are about 40 Naikan centers in Japan, where you can go and train to obtain a more humble relationship with life (there are also a few centers in Europe; Germany and Austria, among others).

Naikan was developed by Ishin Yoshimoto (1916–88) during the 1940s. The foundation is to reflect over and evaluate oneself and one's actions and their repercussions. The word "naikan" means "to look inward," or, in somewhat more poetically, "to see oneself through the eyes of the soul." The basic thought is that life itself holds an infinite consciousness and love.

Practicing naikan means taking a daily look at your own thoughts and actions so that you eventually may experience how blessed you are on life. The gratitude will then follow on its own. We humans often begin on the wrong end—in other words, we begin with the gratitude, and the result is often only outer observations. To follow naikan means observing things and events with a loving eye—then gratitude will rise from our inner self.

Naikan may sound easy as it is described, but in reality it demands immense self-discipline The practice peels off all the parts of us that do not carry fruit or give us nutrition.

Wabi sabi, naikan, and life itself don't demand anything of us—we are allowed to be the way we want. But making the journey toward peace of mind and satisfaction in life demands maturity and self-reflection. And so we have to take a look at our failures and mistakes, or as they say in the twelve-step program: "I am going through a radical and fearless moral inventory of myself." Naikan peels away all fake myths and lets us stay away from egocentric and self-centered actions.

In the beginning I had trouble with naikan myself, and this was because of a phenomenon that had spread like wildfire through the movement I had worked with for the past 20 years—that which is called "personal development." The phenomenon is about always keeping yourself in the center and observing everything from your own perspective—to always emphasize "I want," "I shall," "I have a right to," "My goals are. . ." This movement has most likely now met its culmination, and we are starting to realize that we are not going anywhere, but rather that life is here and now. More and more people are starting to embrace the fact that we are here to serve in life and nothing else, and that it is a great gift to be able to do so.

Personally, I finally realized that much of what I succeeded in was manifested with positive thoughts that remained quite flat and soulless. What really gives life meaning is to serve life as a whole. Life is rich when I get up in the morning and ask myself the question: "How can I *serve* life today?" Instead of asking, "What *do I want* today?"

What I have come to understand from wabi sabi and naikan is that nothing is more valuable than peace of mind and freedom of mind. When the ambitious part of me shouts, "I want more!" or "I want something better!", the truth is that what we really need to want more of is ourselves. If we want more love, we have to give more love. If we want peace, we have to have peace of mind. If we want serenity, we have to accept things as they are and not be at war with life.

Do we not deserve things? Yes, we deserve our longings, our wishes for life; but we cannot forget the road there. We are often so fixated on the goal that we forget the journey, and too often we fail to see the flowers that grow along the road. I have reached almost all of the goals I had set for my life, and of course I am happy about that, but the road to reach them could have been easier and more comfortable if I had been less demanding.

A couple of years ago I was with a group of feng-shui consultants in China. We were visiting Beijing one day. It was warm and dirty, and we were all hungry. We found a restaurant and walked in. Many of us thought the food was poor, and we complained about our meal. Then suddenly one of my colleagues said, "This conversation is making me so tired. Can we not be happy that we are full?"

The rest of us retracted and quieted. I have previously talked about what a haikumoment is (see page 16), and this was one of those moments. I am so grateful for those words. It gave me something to think about, and I remained quiet with my thoughts. When we left the restaurant, I saw a man looking through a dumpster for food. That was another haikumoment. I decided then and there to never again complain about food.

Of course there are certain days when I am not alert and I end up on a self-obsessed path where everything circles around me. But the meeting with wabi sabi and naikan has made such a significant impression on me that I often react before I have been on the path for too long.

One night my 9-year-old daughter slept beside my husband and me. She thinks it's cozy, and if it wasn't for the fact that my husband and I don't sleep well with her lying next to us, we would let her do it more often. I thought a lot about naikan before I fell asleep that night. I slept poorly because my daughter wouldn't lie still, but kept scratching herself endlessly. I was going crazy over the lack of sleep and was close to carrying her back to her own bed. Then I suddenly realized that I was so focused on myself and my sleep that I forgot that I could easily help my daughter if I just went to get her cream against itching. A few minutes later we were both sleeping soundly.

An exercise in reverence and humility

This exercise is part of the Japanese humility training naikan.

Choose five key people in your life. It is wise to begin with your mother, no matter what your relationship with her may be. Let each step take 15 minutes and observe each step as life-affirming and positive.

Step 1:

Sit in silence without distractions. Think about one person close to you.

What has this person given you?

What have you given this person?

What problems and difficulties have you given this person?

Step 2:

Reflect over what you learned from the answers you gave to the questions above. Can you share the gratitude for what this person has given you with him or her? If you feel bad, then forgive yourself for the problems you may have caused, but learn from them while you let them go.

Naikan is about serving life, and when we serve life we also serve ourselves. It is such a freeing feeling when the tenderness and service win over the self-obsession. In those moments, life is at its very best.

A couple of weeks ago I attended a course, and the farm we were going to looked great in the pictures. When we arrived, it turned out that we all had to share rooms, the shower was separate, and we had to help with food preparations.

I had a whole list of reasons why I should have a room of my own, a shower in my room, and not have to prepare my own food when I went to a seminar. I was simply mad and bitter. I found the man who owned the farm and started to explain to him why I needed a room of my own. He looked at me with alert eyes and said what I absolutely did not want to hear: "I think it might be good for you to share a room with the others."

I drew a deep breath and took a moment to think, and to my horrid surprise, I felt in my heart that he was right. I laughed as I walked away.

The seminar turned out great—it was wonderful to prepare the food all together, and at nighttime, I had the most comfortable feeling in my chest as I lay there listening to my friend snoring above me. I experienced a sense of belonging with my roommates and a deep honor to be a part of that experience.

A few days later, I had the opportunity to meet a 16-year-old boy who placed everything in an even greater perspective. This boy has a disease that is causing him to lose more of his vision and hearing each year. Within a few years, he will be almost deaf and may be completely blind—he will live in a world that is both dark and quiet.

Often something develops in people who are put to such tests by life. I think this young man will give the world a great gift. He carried a deep sensitivity, and you could see in his entire being that he was accepting his situation. He will have a lot to teach his fellow human beings.

The greatest lesson that naikan can teach us is finding a way to deal with things that we cannot change. It will always be painful, but we can make it easier or harder on ourselves.

I have had trouble accepting some things in my life, and one of them was a situation that gave me a headache for 18 months. Aches can be terribly testing when we are not used to living with them. After 18 months, I came to a point where I was forced to accept the ache. I told myself: "It is here; there is nothing more you can do . ."

I had tried everything. The next step was to rest in the ache, to stop trying to make it go away or change, and rather just let it be—not give it as much focus, and direct my attention on everything around me instead. After a few weeks, the headache disappeared.

Looking back now, I am immensely grateful for this experience, because I know that aches, pain, sorrow, and despair are part of life and always will be. So why fight so desperately, when this, just like everything else in life, is fleeting?

To understand naikan on a deeper level, we are going to ask three important questions that lead us toward a more humble relationship with life:

- What has life given me?
- What have I given life?
- What kinds of problems and difficulties have I created in life?

The first time I did this exercise, the last question puzzled me. I was trained to always try to find the positive and to see only the good things I had created. Was I now to start feeling guilty and feel bad abut my actions? I have for a long time seen guilt as a bad emotion that you should rid yourself of as soon as possible. It was not until my meeting with naikan that I understood that guilt and a bad conscience have life-affirming qualities. They are guiding principles— innate barriers in us that prevent us from doing whatever we please. In particular, those that may harm others or ourselves.

You should see guilt and conscience as signal lights, because what they are really showing us is a string of unsatisfied needs that need to be met. For instance, the need for closeness, care, and dignity—needs all people share.

It is not until we are able to recognize the problems and difficulties we create in life that we can humbly relate to them in a new way. Naikan leaves the ego behind and sees everything in its entirety, sees life in a larger perspective. When I discover the damages and failures I bring into, for instance, my marriage, I have an easier time being humble in my relationship with my partner. It is also easier for me to accept his/her peculiarities. When I get annoyed at other people, my naikan voice will say: "I forgive you for not being as perfect as I want you to be." Once that is said, all the pieces fall into place around me. Because that is often exactly where the issue lies: We want all people to be perfect.

There is actually a way to make people as wonderful as we want them to be, and that is by giving them loving attention. Then their positive sides will emerge. When we instead choose to see all of their failures and wrongs, they do not get the opportunity to show their other sides. We really need to be what we want to experience.

> If you judge people, you have no time to love them.
>
> MOTHER TERESA

Human Meetings

Ring the bells that can still ring. Forget your perfect offering.
There is a crack in everything. That's how the light gets in.

LEONARD COHEN

To bring wabi sabi into your human relationships is both a relief and a challenge, because if there is a place in life where all of our inner perceptions are put to the test, it is in our relationships with others. In meeting with other people, they mirror our deep longings and our inner wounds, but also our superficiality and our shortcomings.

My own experiences with relationships are very mixed. I will be the first to admit that this part of my life is not what I have viewed as the easiest, and at times, my trust has been put to serious tests. I didn't get a lot of free knowledge from my childhood of how relationships should work—rather, I have had to build each piece. Not until wabi sabi entered my life was I really able to be at peace in meeting with other people.

I think most people—just like me—have preconceived notions of how things ought to be instead of seeing them as they are. We long for something specific and try to construct the reality so that it will fit us. Wabi sabi allows us to live in reality instead; to both rest in ourselves and to really delve deep into meetings with others; to show who we are and what we carry.

In the context of relationships, we need to once again look at wabi sabi's basic idea Everything is always changing, nothing is perfect, and nothing lasts forever. Therefore you should appreciate and enjoy the people around you while you can. It might feel a bit sad to think like this, but when we realize that everything that surrounds us is transient and that it is given to us as a gift and not a birthright, it suddenly becomes a lot easier to live in it.

Then it is nice to know that it is possible to heal anything through ourselves—even broken relationships. I made peace with my father after he was dead. It was not until then that I really understood what had happened during all those years. I could see life's naked truth instead of my own constructed reality.

Of course we should expect things from people in many contexts. For instance, there have to be behavioral codes between people in places where they need to live close to each other. When I quarrel with my daughters about things at home, for instance, I don't get angry or frustrated nowadays, but I try to be as clear as possible about what I expect from them—which is not much, but they are things that I stand by. If I didn't, life in our home wouldn't be bearable for the *entire* family.

But we also need to learn to see the reason behind things. Wabi sabi can help us with this. We humans don't clutter because we think it is funny, we aren't grumpy in the morning because it give us satisfaction, and we do not drive cars like crazy people because we are idiots. There is a truth behind everything, and if you seek this truth, the peace of mind will follow, and life will be so much easier.

There is a timeless truth about humans, and it says that all humans behave well if their needs are met. You do not scream if you are satisfied; you do not fight, and you do not lie. Wabi sabi allows us to seek out the needs in each other and ourselves in order to achieve good relationships.

If the person you are talking to doesn't appear to be listening, be patient. It may simply be that he has a small piece of fluff in his ear.

A.A MILNE, FROM *WINNIE THE POOH*

A great danger in life, and especially in relationships is if you start losing yourself in opinions and views on everything. Wabi sabi trains our ability to let those things go and to rest in ourselves without having words or thoughts about everything around us. When we rest in ourselves, an inner power and strength will come out that shows us what is important and what is not. It is enough to know what is

important for me and to have the ability to place it in a greater perspective. I do not have to meddle in other people's choices. As someone once said: "Everyone has views, just like everyone has a nose, but that doesn't mean I have to be picking yours."

If you feel that you have a lack of energy, you should search yourself about precisely this. My experience is that I have lost great amounts of energy through having opinions about things that had nothing to do with me. Wabi sabi has taught me to observe people from the following perspective: You can be exactly as you wish; I can like you with all your imperfections and peculiarities.

When you rest in yourself, you become a more attractive human being, and that will attract others to rest in your proximity. The more strained you are, the more strained the people around you will be as well. I am sure you have experienced this when you meet a person who is a chatterbox—your own system will react and want to get away.

No matter what people may subject you to, you can learn to rest in the situation. You will never be able to change others through reprimanding or, even less, criticizing their actions. This will give rather the opposite effect. On the other hand, a well-chosen truth from the heart can change people.

A while back, I was reprimanded heavily by a man who had been annoyed with me for quite some time. He wasn't doing especially well, and I understood that much of what he was saying wasn't really meant for me, but I could also hear that much of what he was saying was warranted. If I had not practiced resting and really listening, I most likely would have shut off, yelled back, felt violated, or perceived myself as completely useless. But I listened, rested, and considered the things I needed to change. I did not feel any anger against him, and I have no trouble meeting him today.

When you rest in what is going on, you mentally lower your shoulders, and you gain access to a well of complete wisdom. It is a well that contains all answers and all solutions. When you are there, you always know what the best solution is. There you can find the link between all humans and situations—almost like a virtual internet that can supply you with all information imaginable.

When I rest consciously, I see myself from the outside, kind of like seeing my life on a movie screen with me as an actor. I observe what the person is doing; I see what the roles of the other actors are. I can often tell where the situation is going and steer the course of action in the right direction. When I rest consciously, I do not say much, but what I do say is all the more important. And more than anything, I know when I should say something and when I should not. There are no given answers—this is a wisdom wabi sabi has given me. But if you follow life's spontaneous river and allow yourself to rest, you will get to the right place. Maybe not exactly where you had imagined, but always in the right place.

I live with a man that is a true wabi sabi being. He is easy and light like unrefined sugar. He would never follow a fashion trend or group pressure or try to make a certain impression on people—he is who he is, and he always rests in himself. At times he is like an undisturbed child, which has often annoyed me, as I have been so complicated and pretentious. To make him happy is the easiest thing in the world; he has no high demands. He can definitely love certain things, but he takes cares of them, and he would never buy anything that he doesn't know for sure that he really would use.

I have not always been able to see him this way. I have often been so stuck in my own ego that I have missed the beautiful gift he has. When one approaches him, one does not always get what one wanted, but always what they needed—and that is exactly what wabi sabi is.

People are like stained glass windows. They sparkle and shine when the sun is out, but when the darkness sets in, their true beauty is revealed only if there is a light from within.

ELISABETH KUBLER-ROSS

With an honest look at oneself, one often realizes how self-centered one's reality is. The difference between loving attention and self-centration is the difference between living with an open and a closed heart. Naikan has been a relief for me to rest in. When you look at reality with loving, open eyes, it is so much more beautiful.

The ability to listen with your heart is an art few master. If this ability were to develop, many more relationships would be healed much more rapidly. There are few things that hurt so much as when I can tell that I am not listening to my children. I can feel when they want my attention, but too often, I notice too late. I try to apologize when I discover my mistake, to show them that they deserve to be heard, even if I was not aware enough.

When we really listen, without moving ahead in a story, something opens in the other person. Maybe that is the part of the heart that binds us all, and that part withers when we stop listening.

Today, many relationships are maintained through SMS and quickly forwarded messages of the type, "I care about you and if you resend this message within ten minutes you will have more happiness in your life." But wabi sabi's advice about taking a moment with someone one you care about to drink a cup of tea without affectedness is, in my opinion, so much more valuable than these quick, grand assurances. (Drinking tea is a central part of the Japanese culture—tea and friends go hand in hand!)

Unpretentious, unstressed meals are another phenomenon we should try to maintain. When I was a child, we could visit one another unannounced. It was a wonderful feeling to be able to sit down on someone's kitchen sofa and just talk for a while, drink a glass of lemonade and, at times, just observe while someone was doing their daily chores, like washing dishes or ironing. It was a time where everything was moving slower, and humans were generally less pretentious. Today, we get quite stressed if people are coming to visit—we book it in our calendars and make sure that we have something to offer them at home. But really, we are all longing for something completely different. Wabi sabi doesn't take us back in time, but it allows us to prioritize differently and be more spontaneous.

The naikan teacher Gregg Krech describes the difference between the self-centered human being and the lovingly attentive human being the following way:

Self-centered human being:	Humbly attentive human being
Takes things for granted	Says thank you
Forgives their partner	Asks for forgiveness
Decides their partner's goals	Supports the goals of his/her partner
Sees their partner's faults and shortcomings	Supports the goals the partner chooses
Demands their rights	Recognizes everything as gifts
"How can my partner be more loving?"	"How can I be more loving?"
"What am I not receiving from my partner?"	"What do I receive from my partner?"
"Which problems is my partner giving me?"	"What problems do I give my partner?"
"This is how I think my partner should change."	"This is how I need to change."
"My troubles are because of my partner"	"In what ways do I cause my own problems?"
"I give so much and get so little in return."	"I give so little and receive so much."
"What can my partner do for me?"	"What can I do for my partner?"
"If he/she really loved me . . ."	"If I really love him/her. . ."
"My partner should do an exercise like this."	"I should do an exercise like this more often."

To turn on the light in other people

> What does is mean to flirt? It is a way to take care of the planet. Because when you feel happy, fantastic, and wonderful, you create the same feeling in everyone that surrounds you.
>
> MAMA GENA

If I were to give you one more tip about relationships and people around you, it would be to flirt more! Nothing can turn on the inner light in other people and in us like a healthy flirt!

With flirting, I do not mean working to make a specific person sexually attracted to us. No, what I mean is the special art of making everyone that surrounds you feel good. This is an ancient art.

The relationship therapist Mama Gena (Regena Thomashauer), who is one of my role models, talks about flirting in a way that brings it to a whole new level. A level where all human beings feel really good. I use flirting as often as I can, and I have discovered that it has a magic effect in meetings with people. The art lies in creating an invisible reaction that lights people's life energy. In order to do so, you first need to light your own life energy, and that can be done in seconds if you are well-trained.

I saw a movie on TV where two colleagues always fought. It was about a woman and a man that had become stuck in a bad dynamic, and couldn't work together. The situation was spiraling out of control. In a scene where they are trying to agree on how a product should be sold, they get nowhere. Then you see how the woman suddenly thinks for a second and puts everything on one card: She starts flirting with the man. After a couple of minutes, she has changed the entire situation and the mood is completely different. After awhile, they have solved the work situation and they are both confused—but happy. Not to mention the fact that the flirtation resulted in a real friendship.

If you know this art you can see how people change right before your very eyes!

How to do this?

It is not hard, but it does demand some practice.

First, you have to realize that you are exciting and attractive. Then you are going to quickly transport this energy to the other person with your eyes. The intention is to see the other as exciting and attractive and confirm this with your own energy. On a spiritual level, it could be explained the following way: "The highest in me sees the highest in you." But on a physical level, it needs to be spiced with humor and warmth. You also need a ton of life-affirming confidence to succeed.

I was almost called in for a new inspection of my car because of a small, trivial thing a while back. I was about to get really annoyed with the inspector when I quickly realized how that would be a waste of energy. I tried to talk nicely and rest in the situation instead. And then it suddenly occurred to me that I could try flirting. I took a deep breath and told myself that I was exciting and attractive—and that he was as well.

After five minutes he had fixed the minor problem with my car and I didn't have to go through further inspections. I felt great when I left, and I am certain that he did as well—a sign that the flirtation succeeded!

I do have to mention a few warnings though, when it comes to flirting. Mainly these are about always threading carefully and slowly; finding the right approach and making sure that you have the right intentions. Wanting to see the best in other people and to see them as exciting and attractive is a good intention.

But if you intentionally choose a few people that you flirt excessively with or if you start "pouring out" sexual energy on people in the workplace for instance, it can all go overboard. Wabi sabi always follows the idea of "less is more," and flirting has to be done with humor and warmth and should not be a way of seducing or scaring people away.

As long as you do not hurt anyone, flirting is fine. I flirt with anything—men, women, old, young, my children, my ducks, and my potted plants. As I mentioned, it does take practice and self-discipline, but the practice in itself is fun and calming. It makes us blossom.

> When women are allowed to blossom, that favors the entire community, and coming generations will have a better start in life.
>
> KOFI ANNAN

Unity and balance

The balance between the masculine and the feminine is a vital prerequisite for life. This is not a dualistic idea that separates; it is a way of understanding that the world is created with contradictory phenomenon. In the moment of creation, everything came to be in coupled opposites and symmetry, which created a perfect balance. Everything has its opposite—protons have electrons; uphill has downhill; everything has a cosmic synergy. Matter is yang (the masculine) and anti-matter is yin (the feminine). This theory is important because it shows how balance on earth can only exist when opposing powers connect harmoniously and create a unity.

The materialistic part of our existence has gotten such emphasis, and it needs to be weighed up against the inner worlds. Yin and yang are not the same as man and woman, but the traits are coded in various ways in our physical bodies. Women in general have a larger portion of yin in their bodies; therefore they need to come forth more to strengthen the feminine power in current society. This will also be easier if one generally allows oneself to relax and rest in one's original power.

Men and women's soulful traits are different, even though there are, of course, exceptions. Women seek love more than a man does. Men often seek freedom more than love. That doesn't mean that these things are not important for both men and women.

In order to create unity and balance, we need to rest in our authentic soul power—where women need to go deeper into love, wild nature power, dedication, and flow; and men need to go deeper into silence, presence, power, and depth.

The wise old woman wabi sabi encourages her daughters to rest, rest, and rest some more, so that the natural healing power can arise once more. Women are born with bodies that can nurture and give life. Wabi sabi encourages us to reconcile with wisdom in order to help the earth heal and give humanity their faith in survival once again.

On the one hand, wabi sabi tells us that we are fantastic just the

way we are—she enjoys us in every moment, like a tender mother. On the other hand, her presence makes us want to become better people; live with dignity and with care. Not because she demands it, but because we realize the depth of her wisdom.

This has made me want to know as much as possible about the feminine healing power and about the wild nature power that lives inside the female body. A power that few show today; that many fear and that, historically, has been suppressed and denied. And unfortunately, not only historically: Today, women are forced to hide their bodies, and women are sold, genitally mutilated, and killed because of their sex. The female wild nature power is clearly terrifying.

It is the right of every woman to take this nature power back and to regain her sexuality in a dignified way. There is too little dignity in how sexuality has been exposed up until now. Sexuality is a call for life, and if it is awakened in the right way, there is an abundance of life power to be received from it. This does not absolutely depend on sharing your life with someone.

Wabi sabi trains us to see things as gifts and not rights, but our sexuality is one of the few real rights we have. And this right in itself is an amazing gift!

The feminine sexual power is like the inner earth—hot and deep and filled with powerful magma—and it might not be that surprising then that people have tried to crush it. The woman is the one of the two parties that fills with an energy within during orgasm—men, on the other hand, lose energy.

In order for a women to open her body in complete surrender, she needs to trust her partner. There needs to be a deep and strong closeness for the female power to blossom fully, and few men have this ability. In their defense, it should be said that few women have the ability to open up in this way.

Wabi sabi trains our ability to enter the deep in one another—enter a deep rest, where the authentic power exists. The power doesn't show when every wrong and failure is in focus, but rather when we love what we see unconditionally.

Few things can tear down an intimate relationship like conditions: "I love you if . . . ", "If you do not do this then . . ." The unconditional love lets you be who you are; it says, "I will always be here for you." This is my relationship with wabi sabi—I can always trust that she will be there, even on the days when I stray from my path.

Unity is about much more than just the meeting between the feminine and masculine powers. It is also about a meeting between religions, cultures, and a joint universe. It is time that we realize that we are part of this earth; it is not separate from us. We are all a part of one whole, and every breath links us together.

In meeting with wabi sabi, I realized that all of the things I try to keep away from myself are actually parts of me. I am part of the world's greed and exploitation of the earth's resources. But I am also part of the unconditional and all-consuming love. I will always be bound to everything around me—I can choose to see this unity or I can remain in the illusion that all things are separate. The choice is mine.

Everything we take for granted will sooner or later be taken away from us. And all we will be left with is a "tone" of ourselves. Maybe this tone is the human soul? As long as I walk this earth, I can choose if my tone will vibrate beautifully, and I can choose if it will vibrate with others in a beautiful symphony.

The masculine power (yang) is traditionally viewed as:

development
advancing
intent objectives
awareness
direction
structure strategy
stability
organization
self-discipline clear
 guidelines
performance
"doing" speed bravery

The feminine power (yin) is traditionally viewed as:

dedication flow
openness flexibility
nurture tenderness
humility timeless beauty
sensibility homecoming
healing empathy
"being" boundlessness
sensuality enjoyment
wild force of nature
death and rebirth
deep ecstasy

Powers that are both masculine and feminine:

unconditional
love
grace
mercy
integrity
strength
courage
vulnerability
freedom
independence
limiting
sexuality

The wild power within us

You were wild and free, do not let them tame you.

ANONYMOUS

There is a wild and uncontrolled natural power living inside each and every one of us. It is the part of us that does not follow the norms, laws, and conventions, and that is completely uninterested in how it is perceived by others. We are all part of nature, and we have, just like nature, the ability to sometimes be silent and organized, and sometimes absolutely chaotic. This is more prevalent in a female body than the man's, I think. In eastern cultures, they say that the female body has a stronger connection to nature (among other things, this includes the moon phases) and that the female biological system is easier to influence.

It may be easy to think that wabi sabi is a silent and content philosophy, but in reality it takes us further into the depth of nature's wisdom—and nature is not always calm; it is rather quite violent in its expression. It can be both chaotic and angry, wrenching and full of mischief. The timeless wisdom allows us to recognize that we are like this as well. To be human is to embrace all of this, and wabi sabi allows us to be at peace with it.

Nothing is perfect, nothing lasts forever—sometimes it's sunny and sometimes it's dark and cold. Sometimes nature smells wonderful; sometimes it smells like rot—and that is what is so fascinating about life, humans, and nature. Do not attempt to make life different than what it is! Rest in it and observe what is going on; then, life will have a natural solution for most things. There will be sun after rain, of that we can be certain.

The wild natural power within us will also take us to the wild part of ourselves, where the passion, creativity, desire and sexuality live. Many people use a desperate amount of energy on suppressing this part of themselves. I have done it myself and I know the price: It stagnates, it's grey, and everything becomes okay. Life loses its spark; the spark that is so important in order for us to get up in the morning and see every opportunity in life.

When you walk without your spark, all doors close. If the doors have been closed for a long time, we often need both tears and pain to open them once more—but to find our natural power again is our own personal earthquake.

If all humans were to start singing more, many of the earth's troubles would cease to exist; I am convinced of that. If we were to dance more, even more of the troubles would cease still. I am talking of free dance—a dance without rules that takes us to layers of our inner self, and where the rhythm is allowed to pick the tensions away. I have hosted groups in this kind of dance for years, and I love seeing humans lose control completely and the "absence" of life that slowly but surely lets the rhythm lead the way to the life power and the wild nature.

Once I asked a woman how she felt after the dance, and she said: "I'm feeling shamelessly good!" I treasured these words deep within me. What does it mean to feel shamelessly good? It means to step outside one's boundaries, one's own and others' expectations; to feel free, crazy, happy, and without shame. It is to give in with humor and warmth, be present in the wild nature power, and let it carry you for a while.

We wouldn't feel well if we were to live in this wild nature power every second of every day—we would be exhausted—but if it never existed, the will to live would cease. We need access to it, to know that the doors are open, and when we need to enter.

All of my adult life I have worked to encourage humans to engage fully in life. I have a strong wish to see humans conquer their lives and live them to the fullest. I want to see the world dance; see the world free, beautiful, and untamed. To me, untamed means that humans are not kept in check, but do not harm each other either.

I remember a guy that was part of a youth group I managed about 15 years ago. He loved his guitar—he sang and played; he had the guitar with him everywhere and always. It was his life. But there was a dilemma: He was the only son, and the family owned a large farm that he was supposed to take over. He often joked about it, but it didn't take long to see his sorrow and despair behind the jokes. He didn't want to be a farmer; he wanted to be a musician.

About 10 other teens and I sat together and listened to him play and joke, and we sympathized with him to the extent that at the end of it, he broke down and admitted his pain and powerlessness. He cried like a child, and I told him that he had to take his guitar and go out there in the world; there was no other solution.

We have to go there our hearts lead us. That is the timeless wisdom. How we choose to live is part of the great fabric of human consciousness. You should see it as a gift to humanity.

For women who do not dare to dance, do not dare to let go, I sometimes say: "Do it for the women who still wear the veil; do it for the two million girls suffering genital mutilation every year; do it for those who will be stoned to death just so that their wild force of nature will not be seen!" We act for each other as well. Our contribution is important. If you cannot open your heart for your own sake, do it for all of the children in the world that walk alone.

When we realize that we are part of the great human fabric, something usually opens, and we understand that there is nothing we can do for someone or against someone that does not affect us. This is a deep and timeless wisdom.

Devotion

Have you ever noticed how happy people are often very spontaneous? They want to participate in what is going on. They are not
afraid to seem nutty if it makes their lives happier. They dance, even
if they do not know the steps and have two left feet. They sing, even
if it is out of tune and they do not remember the lyrics. They do
the things that bring forth happiness without considering what the
world around them might think. They are happy to laugh and laugh
freely.

Happy people might seem like nutjobs, but they are happy
nutjobs. Can you make a better choice than choosing happiness?
Be happy.

JOHN MORTON, FROM *YOU ARE THE BLESSINGS*

Wabi sabi has taught me devotion to life. For that I am forever grateful. Nowadays I rarely think of where I am going, what is expected
of me, or what my next step should be. I have visions, but I do not
know how they will manifest: I trust that life will show me. Instead
I try to focus on deep breaths, relaxing, and going with the flow. It
can be really difficult at times, and in that case it will just have to be
hard—I do not think much about that either.

To rest in what is happening and to find help in dance has become
my way of easing my existence. What is your way?

The art of indulging is a gift; a gift that should be shared. We are
born with it, but are too often influenced by another sort of life, where
this gift doesn't show. If we train it—through rest—it will automati-

69

cally step forth as a longing for life; a longing for wanting to live. This longing is always there in us, even when it is at its darkest. When we rest in what is happening, the devotion will come creeping in.

Devotion never takes up much space; it is like wabi sabi—modest and giving in its nature. In traditional religious contexts, devotion is not much discussed—rather, delight and enthusiasm. These words differ slightly in meaning. Delight and enthusiasm are grander words and they refer to ecstasy, great excitement, delirium, and exaltation; while devotion is softer and calmer and refers to forgiveness, tenderness, and love. The word also holds a hint of self-sacrifice, which I think is especially important nowadays. We can no longer just think of ourselves; we have to take a step back in order to let something else walk ahead—sometimes we have to sacrifice something for something bigger.

Devotion is about the willingness to meet life and be open to what is. The road there is about lowering your shoulders, resting in what is happening, and letting the body open up.

Sometimes you may have to fool yourself into getting where you want. The brain, which controls our bodily functions, cannot separate between truth and lies—it will only do as it is told. Therefore we may sometimes need to do something "as if" to make it understand and send new instructions: Dance as if we were a little crazy, open up as if we felt fantastic, sing as if we were the world's best singer . . . The timeless wisdom never minds a dose of happy craziness.

THE OPEN WINDOW

Inside each of us
there awaits a wonder
full
spirit of freedom

she waits
to dance
in the rooms
of our heart
that are closed

dark and cluttered
she waits
to dance
in the spaces
where negative feelings
have build barricades

and stock-piled weapons
she waits
to dance
in the corners
where we still

do not believe in our goodness
inside each of us
there awaits
a wonder
full

spirit of freedom
she will lift light feet
and make glad songs
within us
on the day we open the door of ego
and let the enemies stomp out

JOYCE RUPP, FROM THE STAR IN MY HEART

When life does not turn out as expected

Life does not disappoint us, it is our expectations for life that does.

GREG KRECH

We have all experienced disappointment. We might have felt like we have been served a burden that is too heavy to carry. Personally, I have cursed things that didn't turn out as expected multiple times, and I have cried of the want and longing for happiness; this odd happiness that I felt that everyone else had.

I remember being a child and happiness seemed so distant from our family. Everyone else had dads, money, things—but first and foremost happiness, which I thought every family had, except for mine. That makes me remember how important it is to talk with our children about the things on their minds and how they perceive things.

I am convinced that it is the hunt for this utopian happiness that drives us to do many strange things. We stress ourselves to reach those moments in life when everything is simply good. Wabi sabi teaches us that we definitely can get small moments of euphoria and happiness, but that at the end what really gives us peace of mind and calm is contentment and the ability to enjoy what we have. That doesn't mean that we shouldn't work for things, but we should learn to keep a more sober relationship to this striving.

There is a legend in wabi sabi that is about a man that asks Buddha for guidance. The man says, "I have a good life. I am a farmer, but last year's crops were poor. I have fine children that I am proud of, but they do not do as I wish. My wife is amazing and I love her, but she complains all the time. What should I do?"

Buddha listens patiently and responds after a while: "I cannot help you."

The man is both surprised and angry. "Everyone has problems," Buddha says calmly. "They are about 48 in number and you can of course solve some of them, but then new problems will take their place. Everything you own and love will be taken from you, including your dear and loved ones. Nothing lasts forever and everyone will die in the end, even you. The only problem is: What do you plan on doing about it?"

The man gets very upset about the advice and questions Buddha. He says after a while, "I will help you with your 48 worries, and it is your desire to have no worries . . . ?"

A basic rule in wabi sabi is that nothing is forever. Buddha wanted to help the man realize that life will always have worries, and that it is not who you are, but rather how you deal with it that makes the whole difference. The legend explains that no matter who you are and what you do or do not do, you will always have worries, and that pertains to each and every one of us. It is easy to live with illusions, but you will never be free from your worries and challenges—they are part of life; it will always be that way. The only thing we can do is to learn to accept things as they are. If I had lost a leg, if my wife cheated, if my shares have fallen in value, if my daughter doesn't speak to me—I have no other choice but to accept these things and deal with them in a way that does not hurt myself or others. We are, of course, allowed to get upset, sad, and disappointed, but we can't allow them to eat us alive. Furthermore, it is important to help each other when life gets hard.

Mother Mary comes to me, speaking words of wisdom, let it be.

PAUL MCCARTNEY

In memory of a friend

I once had a neighbor that I very much enjoyed talking to. He was older than me; he was handsome, rich, and skilled in his profession. One would often read about his successes in the papers, and he drove around in fancy cars that made people moan with jealousy. I thought he was nice, and might have been somewhat starstruck by his successes in the beginning. We became friends for life, and with time I found that he was broken on the inside, which made me like him even more. He seemed like he had everything one could want—except love and peace of mind. Women flocked around him, but he never really let love in.

One day he made a fatal mistake that cost him both his job and his reputation. After this followed a string of risk-taking. The last time I saw him was terrible; his life had broken into a thousand pieces. For the first time in our friendship, I was allowed to touch him; he was shaking in my lap and the helplessness I felt was almost unbearable. I realized that I was holding a person who was dying because of a lack of love and warmth; dying from the longing for a living person who would look past his facade. I have never felt as helpless as I did that day.

He later took his own life. In a letter he left behind, he admitted his longing for love. The letter described a longing so deep that I was shaking after reading it. He touched my own vulnerability.

We humans sometimes hide our pain so intensively that it starts eating at us from within. The feminine power and wabi sabi says: Let what you feel flow forward, cry uncontrollably, scream about what feels right, sigh, and move. The body will always be in movement when things are happening inside of it. When we do not allow the body to move, the pain fastens inside our body.

The timeless wisdom also teaches us that some of our soulful paths have to be walked alone. We can ask for support and help to a certain extent, but the last bit we have to do on our own. This is the part of the road that is most painful, but it is also extremely beautiful from a greater perspective. When we have walked far enough, we'll feel the timeless source of grace.

When my friend died, we found a poem by Pär Lagerkvist that he always had with him:

> Earth's most lovely at light's waning.
> All the love the sky's containing
> lies collected in a dusky light
> over the fields, the homes in sight.
>
> All is pure affection, all is soothing.
> Distant shores the Lord himself is smoothing.
> All is close yet all far off, unknown,
> All is given to mankind on loan.
>
> All is mine, and will be taken from me,
> everything will soon be taken from me.
> Trees and clouds, the fields through which I pace.
> I shall journey – lonely, without trace

The legend of the soul's dark night

There is a legend about how to deal with life's dark sides that has left a deep imprint in my heart and that I wish I knew of during my friend's last days. It is about a man who is lost in the woods.

The passage that we all have to get through at certain points in our life is sometimes called "the soul's dark night," and this legend describes a man who is helplessly lost in a forest that is so dark and cold that he almost fails to find his way out. He is cold and keeps hurting himself on branches and roots. He is hungry and stumbles, and he is starting to realize that he might die in the woods.

He tries to use his last ounce of strength to find a solution, but the more he tries, the blacker the woods get. At the end the man gives up; he falls to the ground and gives in to the cold.

When the cold has taken his body, he suddenly sees light out of the corner of his eye. He tries to understand where the light is coming from. It turns out that it is from a small cottage that the man had overlooked in his despair. He slowly starts to crawl towards the house.

He reaches the opening where the cottage stands and in the door opening he sees an old woman. She smiles at him as if she had been expecting him. She helps him inside and places him in front of the fireplace. She gives him food and something to drink and nurtures his wounds. She doesn't say anything, but he knows that she knows everything about him. When he is finished eating, she finds a blanket and wraps it around him. Then she lifts his thin body and sits down in the rocking chair in front of the fireplace with him in her lap. He lies like a weak whisper in her arms, and she consoles him. They sit like this all night. She strokes his hair and sings wordless songs for him. During the night the man becomes smaller and smaller. Layer by layer leaves his body, and when he is finally small enough that she can hold him in one hand, she rises from the rocking chair, opens the window, and from her hand soars a bird . . .

This legend teaches us that it is when life is at its darkest that light appears. It also teaches us that the best way of finding a solution is to give in to life and let life's self-healing powers do the job. The more we look, the less we find. There is mercy and compassion in this universe for the one who is ready to get down to their knees and give in.

Furthermore, the legend teaches us concrete things like how we need to consume food and water before we can find the light. A body suffering from dehydration is scared and sends out despair. The woman in the legend is the soul of wabi sabi, the motherly mercy and compassion, the certainty in our hearts that we will always return to. She never offers good advice, she never criticizes, and she never takes away our pain, but she is there at all times. The easiest way to experience her is to wrap the blanket around ourselves and hold ourselves in warmth, tenderness, and love; then her presence will expand.

The legend teaches us another thing as well, and that is that we need each other. We need to practice our ability to be good to ourselves and one another. Rather a smile too many that none at all. A common word, a warming hand, and an open heart is all we need to take part in the source of grace.

We will have to learn a way to approach problems that involves sitting down in calm and quiet and looking at the problems with tenderness, and they will soon fly out the window . . .

The meeting with my friend taught me another very important thing about life—namely how dangerous it is to bind your longing for (for instance) love and peace of mind to something specific, like meeting a specific man or woman, a special profession, good health, or similar.

Wabi sabi teaches us to let go of our dependence on things and rather go deeper into what is. Instead of desperately longing for an experience of intimacy and closeness with a specific person, we should relax and go into the intimacy and closeness that already exists around us, even if it's just the wind or a fruit lying on the table in front of us . . . What we long for always exists, but not outside; rather, inside of our hearts. We should not cross the river to get water. When we finally find our piece of mind and intimacy with life, you will suddenly find a party on the other side that wants to share it with us, because by then we have become immensely attractive.

Think about:
• In which areas of my life do I need support?
• In which areas should I be a support?

The trivial things

A very puzzling phenomenon is how much we focus on things that really don't deserve our attention. Most often we see them and are upset by them because we are generally in a bad place, and it is here wabi sabi can help. Once again it is all about letting things go and allowing them to be imperfect. There is nothing in wabi sabi that is perfect or that ever will be perfect, so you just have to "let it pass."

As soon as I feel that I am getting annoyed over trivialities, I try to accept what I am seeing without it affecting me or entering into it. I especially try to avoid analyzing it. Everything exists in the fabric of life; it is full of viewpoints, thoughts, and opinions—but just let it exist instead of engaging in everything and losing energy. I should want to call wabi sabi the most energy-efficient life form there is!

We can let go of most of life's dismays, but there are also moments where life demands high stakes, and those moments can end up causing you a lot of pain. But in those times we need to remember that pain in its purest form is always passing.

When wabi sabi uses her full strength, she can strike like lightening. The great mother sees everything, and takes everything under her protective wings, but if she has to roar, she does so with vengeance. Once we've lived with her for a while, she rarely needs to resort to such powerful expressive forms, but before we have learned to listen and loosen our boundaries, there may be times when she needs to be strict with us. This can happen, for instance, when life over and over tries to show us something we choose to ignore, and then at the end of it we end up with a heart attack, a divorce, or some other disaster.

LEAF BY LEAF BY LEAF

Leaf by leaf by leaf
they tumble and fall:
all my haggard hurts

like a cottonwood tree
ever so slowly letting go,
so the heartache of my heart.

there goes a bit of sadness,
now a leaf of anger flies;
then it's the dropping of self-pity.

the leaf of unforgiveness
takes forever to fall,
almost as long as non-trusting.

leaf by leaf by leaf
they fall from my heart,
like a tree in its own time.

old wounds don't heal quickly,
they drop in despairing slowness,
never looking at the clock.

it seems a forever process,
this healing of the hurt,
and I am none too patient.

but a quiet day finally comes
when the old tree with no leaves
is decidedly ready for the new.

and in my waiting heart,
the branches with no leaves
have just a hint of green.

JOYCE RUPP

The twelve steps

God, grant me the serenity to accept the things I cannot change,
Courage to change the things I can, And wisdom to know the
difference.

THE SERENITY PRAYER

Reaching the serenity and enjoyment of wabi sabi is both easy and
hard at the same time. The day we stop fighting life, and rather rest in
everything that happens and accept that life is always changing, it is
easy. But there are difficult moments; moments that are challenging
to deal with on your own—and in those moments we need powerful
tools.

My way of reaching what wabi sabi stands for when life gets hard
is to use the twelve-step method. The method first spread during the
1930s to try to help people deal with problems with alcoholism. I have
had to modify it slightly in order for people to use it, and if you prefer
not to use the word God, you can easily substitute it with love or wisdom. The most important element of the twelve-step process is that
you have a good sense of how you view God.

My way of interpreting the twelve follows (you may find the original version at the back of the book):

The first step is about realizing and admitting to the fact that all of our
lives will sometimes be difficult and that we are powerless to change
this. It is such a relief to accept this fact.

During steps two and three, we need to open ourselves to the possibility of a higher power that may help us and that we are willing to succumb to. When we realize that we do not have control over our lives and the events that take place, a well-deserved rest will emerge (one of wabi sabi's pillars).

When we are at this stage it is easy to move onto step four, which is about the tender soul-searching (which wabi sabi calls naikan). When we rest in a state of surrender, it is easier to see who we are, what we create, and what is our part in our worries.

The next step is to stand behind what we have created in our surroundings that is not life-affirming. Here, it is very important to accept the shortcomings of other people. In wabi sabi, we see this more as human characteristics than as failures or flaws, and judge no one.

During steps six and seven, a process of surrender happens, where we ask the higher power to take care of our worries and our less life-affirming characteristics. We ask to have them removed.

If people around us have experienced pain and despair because of our way of reacting, step eight is especially important; where we make right—as lovingly as we can—our wrongdoings.

During step nine, we seek reconciliation with the events in our lives, and during step ten we continue to search within ourselves.

When we follow this process, a longing is born within us; a longing to continue to deal with life in this way. If we have had people around us as a support, moving onto steps eleven and twelve is easier. They are about finding multiple ways of being in contact with the wisdom, love, God, or whatever we choose as our higher power. For me, dancing has been the solution—I pray through dance, song, and goddess yoga (which is a way of practicing the feminine qualities of our bodies through movement)— but first and foremost I make sure that I surround myself with people that encourage and support me. It also wakens a longing for sharing the wisdom from this journey with the world around us—and this is the last step of the twelve-step program.

The best part of the twelve-step process, besides the result, is the community. And the sense of community is important, because it can be hard to find your way when everything is black as night. There are twelve-step groups and self-help movements all over the country. You may find them through the internet.

Think about:
- What does my life consist of right now?
- What do I wish to embrace?
- What do I need to let go of?

Trust and confidence

I am not good, because that is not possible, I am a person and I exist. Free and happy, except that's not possible.

BODIL MALMSTEN, FROM *PRISET PÅ VATTEN I FINISTERE*

The further one reaches into the subject of wabi sabi, the more evident a timeless truth and beauty becomes. It is a truth that cannot be questioned. It exists within all of us, often buried deep, but few people live in contact with it. Therefore, the silence and reflection is so important in wabi sabi. But where is the silence and quiet today, and why is it so hard to find?

There are moments when I long for silence and quiet, but at other times I am not pulled in that direction, even if that's when I might need it most. There are times when I don't want to hear the truth that exists within me; I do not listen to the voice that knows that the life-affirming feeling exists. Far into this truth the answers to any problem exists. And the wisdom shows us the truth from a greater perspective.

My meeting with wabi sabi has made me realize that what I may, from the outside, perceive as the truth, may not be the truth at all. It is just interpretations in different variations. We construct a way of looking at things that suits us best. We trust our minds and how we perceive the world. But what do we really know?

Our eyes only perceive a small part of all that exists; our noses can only smell scents within a certain area; and our brains only use a fraction of its span . . . But deep inside all of us exists a world where every answer lies, and if we haven't listened to them for a long time, they can really shake us up once we let them reach us.

The reason we preferably do not seek the silence and quiet is that we are afraid to meet ourselves and all of the contradictions we live with. In the silence we have to confront the one thing all humans

share: The fear of surrendering, the fear of not being accepted, the fear of not being good enough, the fear that life won't turn out as we imagined.

Wabi sabi cannot take these fears away from us—nor can she shield us from death or the pain—but she pours us a large glass of trust and support. Wabi sabi carefully carries us through life, towards a larger and more beautiful depth. If we can accept that the fear exists and practice resting in it, we will eventually reach the truth within us. And it is always calm and tender, and knows where to guide us. When you have finally reached this truth, it is hard to resist. If you do, life will become more painful each day.

There was a time when I thought that fear and frustration would disappear if I worked enough on myself and my personal growth. It turns out that this is wrong. I grew up with much loneliness and frustration that life did not give me the things I wanted or that I felt I needed. As long as these fears are a part of this world, they are also a part of me—and these are the emotions I most often find when I surrender to myself in silence. But wabi sabi has taught me to rest in them and not to try to change them. If I allow myself to fall even deeper, I arrive at the deepest depth where I will find trust, faith, and a wisdom that is so comfortable that it makes every journey through the pain like a gift.

To rest in your fears does not mean sitting silent and stiff on a chair or in your bed. When the body is afraid, it wants to move. If you look at animals that are frightened, you can see how they shake and whimper. We need to do this as well: Shake and give our fears room; let the tears come; let the pain be heard. Pain and fear will always pass if they are allowed to surface. However, we may suffer for a very long time—and that is what happens when we do not allow our emotions to surface, but rather let them fester in our systems.

It can also be incredibly freeing to get everything out before another. To share your fears with someone else. Hidden fears will often grow out of proportion.

The amazing ability of wabi sabi is that it does not try to beautify the world, but rather helps us live in it with sober eyes, anchored in the wisdom and love that we hold within. When we climb down into the wisdom, we see that all humans are scared. We all share the same needs, and if we are able to see these needs in ourselves and others, a freeing veil covers us.

When you see another person make bad decisions and you are trained to rest in what you see, you will easily be able to discover which unsatisfied needs hide behind the actions. This doesn't mean that these people should be allowed to hurt us, but it creates an understanding of where they are coming from.

At the end of the 1980s, I worked as a prison officer. There I saw many broken, frightened men that had been turned into "monsters." I especially remember one guy that I was scared of. It was impossible to maintain eye contact with him, and he looked like he was prepared to kill at any given moment. That was exactly what he had done—he had killed his father and stepmother.

For a while, one of my tasks was to oversee phone calls, and I was at one point forced to sit in a small room with him where there was only a small table, two chairs facing each other, and a phone. He was calling his mother, and the resignation they both revealed was painful to witness.

With a hushed voice the mother said to her son: "Do you understand that you may be imprisoned for life for your actions?"

He sat quiet, and finally he said, "If I have to sit in here until I die it will still be worth it."

His eyes met mine and for a short while I saw straight into him.

I saw a wounded soul, and I instinctively felt that if I had been in his shoes I would have chosen the same action as he had. He had gone through things no child should.

That day I made a promise to myself to always try to see past what I want to perceive, and not be prejudiced about things I know nothing about. And the truth is that there is very much I know very little about . . . Wabi sabi never judges.

Serving life and others

How often do we humans really look at each other? For how long can I stare into another person's eyes, and what happens within me when I do? It has always been said that the eyes are the windows to the soul—so why not stay for a while? If married couples could do this once in a while instead of fighting, maybe they wouldn't be forced to go to therapy, but rather they would find the answers to their issues in a closer environment.

When we realize that impermanence and that we won't always have each other, our hearts open and we can let go of each other's flaws. If we "look deeper," we may appreciate what exists around us in all its imperfection.

The trust comes when we stand still and rest in ourselves and see how amazingly intelligently nature has brought us together. Physics will soon be able to prove that everything is bound together in something we may call a web. This web has been described in almost every religion, and the most fantastic part of it is that all religions basically have the same visions. In the future we will therefore be able to see how the religions and science melt together in one large divine truth, and this truth will never be found in heaven, of that we can be certain. It might have been this that Jesus tried to convey when he said: "God's kingdom exists within you."

The wisdom carries the message that life should be like a prayer. To live in the prayer is to be part of weaving the divine web. Personally, it makes me want to live my life as well as I can, so that I can serve life in various ways. I do not expect that I will be perfect, but I expect that life can be good and that it wills me well. Humans are by nature created to serve life—the reason is that we actually want a good world.

To feel slightly imprisoned is to see life as it is and serve it as it comes to us. I know that I will die, I know that none of my relationships will last forever, I know that life will be painful, and I also know that it will be beautiful and joyful at regular intervals. To be slightly imprisoned in trust means to relax and to stop fighting life. We will never receive a promise of how life should be or that it will be easy.

My life has never been as wonderful as it became when I learned to serve life from the deep of my heart. When one walks through life with a serving attitude, it becomes so incredibly rich.

We seek knowledge and we seek wisdom, but we often forget that these things are already in us. To be wise is to be in contact with one's heart and one's soul. When we reach that point, a will to spread this wisdom will automatically rise.

I think of a woman that made it her foremost task to spread joy. She basically succeeded every time. She was even talented enough that she could criticize and reprimand people, and they would appreciate it. With a wide smile she could say to a teenager: "You, wonderful thing, are way too amazing to smoke . . ."

Kindness always has a soft landing and can guide people in a very different direction than prejudice will. In order to act this way, one needs to learn to live with an open heart and to dare to be vulnerable. To serve others and to be kind always carries a risk of being rejected, rebuffed, and belittled, but what does that matter when you think of all of the upsides?

I often meet people who are exhausted, who have given to others all their lives and now feel empty. I view giving as the greatest gift in life, but I have also experienced giving of myself until I feel empty. I have waited to be filled once more, but have been disappointed. But when we serve life and give our gifts in a relaxed manner, we will automatically be refilled. When we give unconditionally and widely, our contact with life deepens.

It is all about embracing life and its beauty until we overflow—it is the overflow of our own lust and passion for life and serving that fills us. It is a timeless wisdom, which is such a large area to discover.

You may serve wherever you are, no matter if you work or not, if you are healthy or not—there is always a part of you that can pay it forward. It doesn't have to be something big; it can be a smile, opening a door, letting a car in front of you, joking with the cashier, or encouraging someone. It demands a willingness and courage (because we can be dismissed or rejected), but it is never dangerous.

Once, I was sitting on the train and listening to two people sitting in front of me. One of them was young and had just become a teacher, full of inspiration and a wish to create. Her visions of what she wanted to achieve with her students made my mother's heart sing. Her conversation partner was an older teacher who kept repeating how the things she was envisioning were not possible to achieve. It was a distressing experience; within 30 minutes, the young teacher's light had gone out as well.

When the colleague went to get coffee I thought to myself: I don't care if I am meddling . . .

I went over to the younger teacher and said, "You are a gift to these children; I would give my right hand to have you as a teacher for my kids."

She looked utterly confused and didn't respond. I am sure she was wondering who I was and what I had heard, but I didn't care. We should never put out the light in each other; we should help each other light up.

The art of dying every day

In almost every single philosophy and religion, they talk about the art of dying. The Zen-Buddhism, which is close to wabi sabi in thought, takes this one step further and encourages us to be born and die in every second. We should let things, situations, and even relationships die. This means that we allow a relationship to die in order for it to be born again. To love like it is one's last minute on Earth makes humans warm and wide open.

In order to learn "to die," we westerners often need to look more closely at the term "death." What can die? Can our bodies die? Can our souls die? What remains?

The first thing wabi sabi shows us is that death is an illusion. Nothing can die and disappear; everything just changes into a different energy. This is something that science also knows. When you throw away your garbage—what does the "away" really mean? Nothing disappears; it is still there but it changes its shape. Everything remains in a cycle.

When nature's wisdom takes care of this, it happens in a tender cycle. When we humans, entangled in our own intellect and our egocentrism, try to take care of it, the cycle is no longer as tender.

When we "die," the body releases our consciousness into the universe. This might be the soul. Science shows that we loose about seven grams of weight when we die, so the soul is seemingly a physical mass.

When I was 19 I was hospitalized in Asia with Vietnamese typhus. Close to nothing in my body functioned anymore, and I will never forget that moment when my consciousness/soul suddenly left my body and whirled around in a never-ending consciousness that in its fantastic form showed the true riches of life.

It was like being in an all-consuming intelligence and a gentle river, where every little part of me was piece of a larger context. It was impossible to remove anything, but everything was changeable.

It was the most wonderful moment of my life, and I still long for the day when I will melt with everything else once more and forget the illusion of a divided world—the greatest lie of all. I am simply another piece of you, and you another piece of me. Anything I do to you, I also do to myself.

So much revealed itself in this moment. The web that binds the entire universe became apparent, and it felt like every breath was a creation in the web. I could weave beautifully and I could weave less beautifully, but everything I created became my own reality. And everything I directed my attention towards grew larger: If I looked at my feet, they grew to larger proportions; if I focused on my loneliness, that became bigger; if I concentrated on the ones I loved, my love grew larger. This way the wisdom crystallized: I chose my own reality.

It took years to really comprehend this experience, and I still have trouble fathoming it completely, even if it's 20 years ago now. It is so easy to glide back into the habitual pattern and the old perceptions. I often return to the idea that the only road to wisdom is consciousness and discipline. Wabi sabi never requires discipline from us, but I need it. Wisdom just stands by us, quiet, until we turn and look at her.

Consciousness and death

We humans are not limited to the laws of nature that we know today, and within a short period of time we will have to write new textbooks with a great amount of new knowledge. Nature science is very close to a breakthrough that will reveal many completely new possibilities.

Meeting death is not uncomfortable in its purest form; it is all of our stories about the meeting that scares us. Death is just another part of life; a transitional phase that leads to a new life. Practicing death means giving up, to capitulate to the course of life. It is the same as resting in consciousness; to rest in one self, and the events that occur around us.

Everything we let die may come back to us in a different form; it is theoretically impossible for anything to disappear. What once has been joined together cannot be separated. It is therefore very important that we learn to be at peace with the things that happen to us. If you were once married and then you divorced, you will never be free from that person—but you can be at peace with the other person in yourself.

Therefore wabi sabi teaches us to gently and carefully fall so deep into the rest that the freeing point is reached. There may come a day when yoga, meditation, antidepressants, and other calming "medications" become unnecessary—not because these things are not good, but because we have learned to rest in everything that happens.

Timeless spirituality

"All matter originates and exists only by virtue of a force... We must assume behind this force the existence of a conscious and intelligent Mind. This Mind is the matrix of all matter."

MAX PLANCK

In wabi sabi exists a deep, a tenderness, an awe, and a respect for life that goes far beyond our great religions. The fantastic thing about wabi sabi is that she never sets demands. Wabi sabi will always be at our side and wait for us, as an old wise lady that has all the time in the world.

If Jesus, Buddha, and Mohammad were to get to know wabi sabi, they would love her and all that she stands for. There is nothing in her that goes against their wisdom. She would never fight with them, but rather give her deepest gifts in complete surrender—just like nature does for us every day and every week, for all our lives, without demanding anything in return. The trees gives us shadow, the water cools us, the ground gives us crops, and never do they ask for anything in return—and just like this is wabi sabi. Timeless, simple, beautiful, and life-giving. Wabi sabi is difficult to dress in words, because no words on earth can do her justice. The more you try, the further you may move away from her.

What we can see all over the world is that the large religions are starting to crack and shake. We live in a time that is contradictory and where much is brought up to the surface. How can we fight wars in God's name? How can we commit brutal honor killings of our daughters if Allah is good?

While the religions are losing much of their power over people, many of us fear the void that remains. Who will protect human life? Will our rituals disappear? Who will take care of the sacred rooms? Who will defend ethics and morals if the voice of the church is weakened? Will we be delivered only to our own perceptions if religions recede?

A while back I spoke to a man who said that he was a "half-believer." He couldn't see how life could have meaning if the guidelines of ethics and love were to disappear. Who would support these guidelines in the community if the church was gone? Would the politicians be able to do it? In this way, the church does maintain an important position.

Wabi sabi is not a religion; I wouldn't even call it a philosophy—it is more of a life wisdom. The silent spirituality is anchored in our hearts, and we can feel when we are close to it. When we have chosen the wrong path, it is gnawing in us.

A community phenomenon we can observe nowadays is a revelation of many contradictions. I think this is a result of two things: The first is that we have been living with delusions, or rather illusions, which we have accepted without questioning. For thousands of years we have trusted authorities that have dictated the truth for us, but we have now entered an age where we have to think for ourselves. The other factor is that we have a great need for a deeper wisdom, silence, and a valuable life. We frantically search for something sustainable; a truth we can trust. This can easily become turbulent.

The Eastern religions often point out that you cannot dress the wisdom teachings in words; if you do, the experience disappears. If you were to ask a Japanese person what wabi sabi is, they might laugh and answer evasively. Not because they do not know the subject, but because they know that it cannot be put into words.

"Emptiness" is a common phrase within the Zen-Buddhism. I would rather choose the word "void." Our entire physical world, the way we know it today, consists of 99.9 percent void. To really grasp what this means we can think of our smallest constituents, the atoms. The chair you are sitting on, the hand that is holding this book, the ground under your feet—99.9 percent void. Even we are mostly a void.

If we compare an atom with a cathedral, the atom core is the same size as a penny and the electron that circles around it is the outer wall of the cathedral; the remainder of the cathedral is still a huge void. It is in this void that the silent spirituality exists, which you cannot describe—but in a curious way, it consists of a divine web that can create life. There has to be an intelligence behind this fact.

Spirituality and science

Wabi sabi and spirituality is hard to measure and research, but one thing we most likely will witness in the future is that science will move towards religion and vise versa. These two subjects have been two aggressive masculine powers for hundreds of years, constantly competing about who's right. It is the deep, gentle, feminine wisdom and the wordless spirituality that will bring them together, because spirituality and research/science belongs together.

If we focus on our history we can see that science in our culture originated in philosophy, and that it was the church that first started to research "scientifically." The separation between spirituality and science happened about 500 years ago, and it was mainly a result of the church's spiritual corruption at the time, where the science that did not correspond to the dogmas of the church was dismissed.

The Polish astronomist Nicolaus Copernicus may be said to have started the separating process when he, in 1543, published a work that described the sun as the center of the universe—not Earth. He knew that it was dangerous to spread this knowledge since it went against the belief of the church of Earth as the center of God's world. Copernicus therefore waited until he was lying on his deathbed to publish his work.

His concern was definitely warranted, for the Inquisition resorted to terrible methods. A Dominican monk was foolhardy enough to defend the thoughts of Copernicus and was immediately burned. The science and research then went underground and not 100 years later, it resurfaced "in freedom." At this time the mathematician and philosopher Rene Descartes stepped forward and stated that one had to use scientific methods to research the credibility of all "truths."

This is when the church and science really broke apart. And it didn't better the situation when Charles Darwin proclaimed that there was no need for divine intervention in human life or in research. He meant that life was about surviving and that was that.

The division of spirituality and science has incited terrible consequences. The technology that has emerged from science has moved the human civilization to a deadly edge, by destroying life on Earth at a furious pace.

We now find ourselves in a very special day and age, where science will need to find a new direction—not back to religion, but rather toward the wisdom of nature and the silent spirituality. This process is already begun—biometrics (see page 103), noetics, and epigenetics are examples of this.

We need to use science to understand how life begins and how the order of nature really works. We do not need science to master nature or to control it as before; rather we need it as a guide into our future.

Most scientists that have entered the deep of nature's wonderful world have a respect, an appreciation, and a wonder over how magnificently everything is bound. Isaac Newton said: "The most beautiful system of the sun, planets, and comets could only proceed from the counsel and dominion of an intelligent being."

On of the world's most famous cell biologists, Bruce Lipton, has told the story of how, when he first understood how the mechanisms of the cell membranes functions, his heart ached and he got teary-eyed in wonder.

Science is now entering new terrain, which will show us our innermost being and also our immortality. Wabi sabi does not view death as we humans often do. She knows nothing lasts forever, but that doesn't mean that it disappears—nothing disappears, everything lives and starts over endlessly. There is no beginning or end. The only thing that happens is that life and things change their shape; life remains, but in a different form. Everything moves in endless cycles.

My fascination for the relation between science and spirituality led me to CERN, the world's largest particle physics laboratory, in Geneva, where they research the construction of atoms and the creation of the universe—in other words, the Big Bang.

Why is it so important to research this? Well, because this is where all of the excitement begins, and it is here that science and spirituality meet. Allowing particles to collide may be the key to understanding the building blocks of the universe.

The spiritual aspect of particle physics is: Where did we come from? What are we doing here? What is the meaning of life and the universe?

The answers we may find through this project may be different from anything we could imagine; it will shake the foundation of modern physics, and we will have to learn to rewrite our textbooks.

In the scientific world, there is no general consensus about what the Big Bang—the creation of our universe—really was, but the main agreeing theories say that it started about 14 billion years ago with a very small unit, maybe not bigger than a pea, but many times warmer than the son and with a massive energy. At some point this unit exploded and equally sized matter and anti-matter emerged. Most of it obliterated, because matter and anti-matter take each other out and create energy. The universe was created from the leftovers of the matter.

It is the so-called void that emerged during the Big Bang that is of interest in this discussion—in other words, the anti-matter; all that we cannot see with our eyes. The spiritual world calls this "the web," "the grid," "the invisible worlds," "the energy field," "the matrix/blueprint"—the pure energy that spurred creation. Religions may call it God, Jehova, Buddha, the Power, or the Singularity.

A Catholic monk, Georges Lemaitre, first expressed the Big Bang theory in 1927. The scientist claimed the theory, cleansed it of religious overtones, and gave it a mathematical expression. The moment of creation itself, however, physics cannot explain—which religions do easily. When you approach the moment of creation, the mathematics, as we know it, fall apart and become meaningless.

The CERN project may even give us proof that the theory of creation put forth in the first Genesis in the Bible might be scientifically possible. The experiment may even convince religious practitioners that physics is God's law. Nature, science, and religion state the same fact: In the moment of creation, contradictory pairs emerged, which meant symmetry; perfect balance. It is sometimes said that nature science and religion do not contradict each other; nature science is just too young to understand religion.

> God finds knowledge like that behind every door.
>
> PIUS XII

There is a warning sign from nature when it comes to atomic research, and it is about the fact that nature normally will not destroy to create—there are wiser ways to solving things. I am convinced that one day humans will be able to master technology in a entirely different way; therefore, the teachings of, for instance biometrics (see page 103), is especially important right now. There is a possibility that we will at some point know how to develop free energy—surely nature can lead us there. Nikola Tesla, one of the world's greatest scientists throughout the times, had a vision of free energy, and with the rapid development of knowledge we are now witnessing this may not be too far away. Just think of the solace of the world if we could find the solution to develop free energy—i.e., the pure energy that be the fuel of tomorrow; 1,000 times richer in energy than nuclear energy; with 100 percent efficiency; without biproducts; without radiation; without pollution. A few grams would be enough to fuel a city with sufficient energy for weeks.

Lasse Zernell, chief editor for the paper *Allt om vetenskap* (All about science), writes in an editorial about the atom research project: "Nobody knows how far we could get in technological development with a complete and functional model for physics. We might be able to develop free energy, make our bodies invincible, travel at faster speed than light, open portals to other universes; yes, everything sci-fi authors may have imagined and more."

One thing that is important to remember in this context is the words of Einstein: "God does not play dice with the universe." There is a plan behind everything.

What will be the next great scientific project? It wouldn't be surprising if science will make some revolutionizing discoveries about our DNA; i.e., the code where all life begins.

The timeless wisdom in wabi sabi has taught me to go out in the world with the following questions in my heart. I am not trying to find the answers to the questions, I rest in them until the asnwers come from deep within.

- Where am I going?
- What is the most important question in my life right now?
- What direction do I want this world to take and how can I help make that happen?
- Can I rest in the occurrences I do not like?
- What is the most loving action I can take?
- Can I let the ones that try to snag me pass on?
- Should I accept or react?
- The disorder I see in this world, what does that mirror in me? How can I deal with it in the gentlest way possible?
- Can I choose tenderness?
- What is my body saying?
- How am I giving my life nurture?
- How am I giving the world around me nurture?
- Am I living in harmony with the cycles of life?
- What do I give to life and what do I receive from life?
- Can I open up and rest in the things that are unsatisfactory?
- Can I rest and forget about all my exertions today?
- Can I live my life as it was a gift today?
- If I am true to myself, what does that mean right now?

Nature's wisdom

Nature does not hurry, yet everything is accomplished.

LAO ZI, FROM DAODEJING

In wabi sabi's innermost caves, all of nature's secrets brood. We can find the answers to all our human questions in nature's intelligence. The further into nature's wisdom we get, the more exciting it gets. It is like Mother Earth, with her 3.8 billion years, is just waiting to show us what she really knows.

Biomimicry

Similarly to wabi sabi, one subject is spreading like wildfire these days—that is biomimicry, the study of how nature creates sustainable life and how we should imitate nature to design in a way that does not tear the system down, but rather create life in the best way possible.

It is incredibly exciting to realize that all the answers we need to have a good life on Earth are out there waiting for us. Wabi sabi always says: *Look closely, look behind, look through—all is not what it seems.* In nature, Mother Nature shows us the solutions.

Biometrics may be used on very high levels. Urban planners, scientists, entrepreneurs, and others now study prairies and coral reefs, among other things, and apply this to cities, industries, and even economies.

One of the first documented biomimics was Leonardo da Vinci, who was inspired by bird wings for his drawings of flying machines at the beginning of the 1500s. The drawings were later used by the Wright brothers when they designed the first airplane at the beginning of the 1900s.

But it is not until the past few decades that biomimicry has really had its breakthrough. Japan, for instance, has used nature as an inspiration for their new express trains: The osprey's shape was modeled to allow a train to turn quickly, and owl feathers have been the basis for creating a train that can move quickly but almost silently.

If you ask nature you will always receive an answer. The problem is that we are not quiet enough to hear the answer!

One of the founders of biometrics is Janine Benyus, who in 1998 wrote the book *Innovation Inspired by Nature,* in which a wide field of biologists, engineers, architects, designers, and entrepreneurs searched nature and found solutions to their problems. Janine Benyus worded what many were already thinking: That nature has already solved the problems we are trying to solve. Why reinvent the wheel? In nature, only the best designs survive; the bad disappears quickly, she says.

Nine founding biometric starting points:

- Nature is driven by solar energy
- Nature returns everything
- Nature only uses the energy it needs
- Nature adjusts the form to its function
- Nature rewards corporation
- Nature gains from diversity
- Nature demands local expertise
- Nature counteracts the excesses from within
- Nature benefits from the power of limitations

Every time humans try to develop something, we basically use the same method. This method could be called "heat, beat, and treat"— i.e., we heat things, push them together, and treat them. What makes this such a hard project, among other things, is that through such development, we only use about four percent of the energy we find, which means that 96 percent of the energy is wasted. In nature, on the other hand, no energy is ever wasted; but rather it moves on into the next cycle.

A lot of exciting research on solar energy today that offers hope. We are about to develop a plane called Solar Impulse that is meant to become the first plane constructed to fly day and night without environmentally damaging fuel. The goal is that it will be able to fly around the world on solar energy alone by 2013.

Recycling and cooperation

Nothing is wasted in nature. Nature only uses the energy it needs. It also has a interesting way of rewarding cooperation that we could learn much from.

Cooperation is one of the foundational words of wabi sabi. We can no longer do our own thing through our existence, for now we know that this will end in disaster. Nature uses diversity, and we need to deepen our understanding of this. Wabi sabi always reminds us of the benefits of diversity, as opposed to mass-produced similarity. We should enjoy the differences and rest in the fact that diversity and originality makes life exciting.

Local knowledge is always used in nature; one simply functions with the things one has in close proximity—one never has to look

very far away. If you look at many of those things that worry us humans these days, the reason is often because we now longer trust local expertise. Decisions are made far from the place it actually concerns. The nurses at a department of a hospital will most likely make better decisions about changes that may affect them than a politician far away from their workplace could.

One interesting phenomenon is that, in places where women have been given micro-loans to solve local problems, this has resulted in more sustainable solutions than when a project had been granted larger sums of money. It would be wrong to say that men are behind every wrong decision made; but rather that the masculine power, which historically has ruled for so long, has part of the responsibility.

We all carry both masculine and feminine power within us. But since women generally carry more feminine than masculine power, we would seemingly create a softer and more sustainable world if women were allowed to decide.

> "The feminine values are the fountain of bliss.
> Know the masculine, Keep to the feminine."
>
> LAO ZI, FROM DAODEJING

It is not until we start asking nature the right questions and we learn to cooperate between various work fields that the right answer will come to us. Janine Benyus writes: "For over 300 years we have studied nature, but we haven't allowed it to teach us. It is about asking the questions in a new way. Biologists have studied why animals act as they do, but they have rarely asked how. There is a large difference between the two. How has been a question for problem solvers, not for researchers."

Now, for instance, we have finally found the answer to how the hummingbird can fly with its heavy body and its seemingly all-too-weak wings. It was not until physicists and biologists decided to cooperate that they realized that it was the wing technique that gave the humming bird its lifting power.

What geese can teach us about cooperation and leadership

I work with leadership development at the Sofia Institute. Nature's wisdom is very important to us at the institute, and we use a cooperation and leadership model based in nature that is about the wisdom geese utilize when they fly in a V-formation. They fly this way so that they can reach a specific goal with the least amount of resistance. If we were to use the wisdom of the geese, the world would be a much better place to live in.

What is the wisdom of the geese?

Every bird flies with its own wings. But by flying in a V-shape, the speed of the herd increases by 71 percent compared to the speed of a single bird flying on its own.
Lesson: Humans that work in a common direction and with a sense of community will reach their goals faster and more easily as they get help from others.

If a goose falls out of formation, it will get back into place as soon as possible in order to benefit from the lifting force of the goose over-current.
Lesson: If we had the same sanity as a goose, we too would stick together and support each other in this way.

When the leading goose is tired, it moves backwards in the formation and another goose takes the lead.
Lesson: It pays to take turns doing the hardest jobs and to divide the leadership roles among each other.

The geese in the far back of the formation will call out to encourage the front geese to keep the speed up.
Lesson: We have to make sure that our calls from the back are encouraging and nothing else.

When a goose is sick or hurt and can no longer fly, two other geese leave the formation to help and protect it. They stay until the goose can either fly again or it dies.
Lesson: We too can protect and support each other. This will also allow us to develop as a group.

Wabi sabi has made me want to be more silent and listen more than talk. I experience that my body—which is part of the wonders of nature—always communicates with me, but unfortunately I do not always want to listen.

Maybe it is human not to hear the whispers of nature, or it is hard because our surroundings are so noisy and loud that the small whispers of nature are not allowed to break through. I do know one thing—that in order to live a good life, I have to listen to what nature and my body are saying. Sometimes, however, you feel powerless when you cannot live by the values nature wisdom provides and that you would like to follow.

A everyday example: I was standing at the grocery store one day and I had promised my children a dessert based on bananas. I was tired and I was short on time. When I went to get my organic bananas as normal, I realized that they didn't have them. It felt wrong to buy bananas where manufacturers had used 2 kilos of pesticides to grow 1 kilo bananas, and where the ground, animals, and humans suffered so that westerners can eat cheap fruit. Still, I bought two bananas.

Right or wrong? The only thing I know is that wabi sabi would never judge or criticize.

A warm loving home

"The secret of contentment is knowing how to enjoy what you have, and to be able to lose all desire for things beyond your reach."

LIN YUTANG

Creating a home with the help of wabi sabi is one of the most beautiful things we can do. A wabi-sabi home is simple and modestly decorated, but with warmth and sincerity. It is first and foremost about valuing things and enjoying their imperfections; to be able to observe an object and not be bothered by the fact that it is not as perfect as you may have wanted it to be.

In wabi sabi, just like in feng shui, it is all about feeling your way and trying various options until you can feel in your stomach that it is right.

A wabi-sabi home is not unkempt and messy; neither is it minimalistic and neatly organized. To live in a wabi-sabi home means living with your things and taking care of them. And this is that much easier if you do not have as much stuff.

An abundance of gadgets creates a mess, demands care, costs money, and prevents us from seeing the important things in life. That doesn't mean that we have to live in poverty, but rather that we should live thoughtfully. If we solely surround ourselves with things we appreciate and use, our lives are simplified and beautified.

The road to a valuable life is about saying no to things and becoming conscious of what matters. So many of us in the Western world would, for instance, be able to work less if we didn't need so many things around us. But the critical point is approaching, and more and more people are starting to realize the extent of what we create with our requests. In wabi sabi, it is not what we have that is important, but rather how we relate to what we have.

A couple of years back, I heard an interesting radio interview with a young man who had recently become an IT-billionaire. He was annoyed by the journalist's constant questions about his life. She was determined to find out why he was still driving around in an old Mazda, living in a small studio apartment, and dressing in simple jeans and T-shirts. Finally he answered: "Why should I change the car I drive just because I have become richer? I love this car, I worked hard to earn the money for it back in the day. And why should I live in a larger apartment than what I need? And why in the world would I change the way I dress now? I am the same person I was before." His answer was breathing wabi sabi inside and out . . .

All of our overconsumption stems from various kinds of fear and from our hunt for the illusion of happiness. "If I don't have my things—then who am I?" We still measure our status in gadgets, but thankfully our future analytics say that this time will soon come to an end. In the future, status will be about quality of life.

Look around you in your home. Of all that you see, what do you need? Remember the cycle of nature when you cleanse it, so that as little as possible is thrown out and as much as possible is recycled. Then prioritize the important rooms, like the bedroom and the kitchen. Treat yourself to a good bed, nice sheets in natural material, utilities of good quality.

When you are faced with things in your home, ask the questions they ask in feng shui:

- Do I like it?
- Do I use it?
- Does it make me feel good?

Be ruthless while doing this. Future analytics say that in the future, we will borrow all the more from each other and rent the things we need. We will come to realize that we do not need our own lawn mower or two cars. Another advantage of renting is that we wouldn't maintain the part of consumption that demands sorting, keeping, and throwing out, which in its turn saves time—and in the future we will prioritize time over money, scientists say.

In wabi sabi, nature materials, craft, and originality is prioritized over mass-produced products. I shop more at flea markets and in secondhand shops, despite the fact that I do not have to economically. One of the reasons for this is that things that were made way back are often of better quality than the mass-produced products of today. Not to mention the fact that mass production happens to a large degree in Asian countries where the working conditions are often both unethical and inhumane.

I will never forget when I, as a feng-shui teacher, studied materials and their history and ended up in the world of cotton. It was a terrible knowledge I had to consume. In the chase for cheap cotton, we have created industries that are completely unworthy workplaces. In order for the low-price chains to keep the prices at such a rate, there are cotton factories where the women are not allowed to go to the bathroom during work hours—as a result, many of them struggle with kidney problems. Today, I would never buy a cheap cotton garment—it shouldn't cost $5.99 to buy a shirt. If it does, you can be sure that the price paid on the other end is extremely high.

Another problem with the cheap clothing production is that the manufacturing is affecting groundwater and waterworks. We should therefore always support the production of organic cotton and, first and foremost, buy clothing that is organically produced.

In wabi sabi, the unique, the personal, and the authentic is brought into focus. We give things a soul, which means that we use them with feeling and understand their worth. A teacup that is comfortable to drink from, an inherited sofa that we sink into—what we love will eventually gain a soul of its own. Think of all the toys the children loved, slept with, and held in their arms; you can't throw those out with an easy heart. (I sometimes see my beloved teddy bear at my grandmother's house, and every time, I straighten his legs and make sure that he is lying comfortably on my old bed. At certain times in my childhood he was everything—things like that live on in our souls.) In wabi sabi, you give things your attention and your gratitude—this way they become life partners, and you can't get rid of life partners.

Choose the simple. Today using a camera or a cellphone has become a science of its own. I try to value the things I have and rarely exchange them. Difficult gadgets pulls us away from wabi sabi.

Another way of heightening the atmosphere in the home is to emphasize natural shapes, preferably wavy. Avoid hard, sharp and cold surfaces. Strengthen the harmony through art. Choose surfaces that feel strong and have a natural shape; shy away from the polished and too shiny.

A journalist asked me if the trend to buy things that are worn and frayed makes us more wabi sabi. This can be a nice beginning, but more importantly, we need to know the reason behind buying, for instance, worn jeans. I think this trend is revealing a hidden side of us. We long for the robust; the things that we know have the ability to deeply nurture our lives, and in the future I think we can allow our-

Things to consider when you wish to create a harmonic home:

- Choose symbols and art that emphasize the simple and closeness to nature.
- Choose natural light to the extent it is possible.
- Create a spot inside or in your garden for reflection.
- Choose rugs and materials that make the room seem calm.
- A ticking clock creates atmosphere.
- Sweep instead of vacuuming.
- Choose the asymmetrical instead of the strict and symmetric.
- Choose soft shapes, spirals, wave and circular shapes, the kind of shapes you can find in nature and in the human body.
- Create a place where you can remember and value your near and dear.
- A gentle waterfall—a fountain, for instance—is calming.

selves to wear things on our own instead of buying something already frayed in the stores. If you want everything at once, then secondhand is a good choice . . .

Feel free to decorate so that the corners disappear—for instance, through placing things right across the corners. This way the room softens. This demands space, but it might be worth it.

Through textiles and curtains you can also create calming rooms; curtains may sift light and this way create softer lines between the walls and windows.

In the future we will see new materials, and it is especially exciting that biometrics will play an important role in this. Maybe we will see textiles that contain the wisdom of the lotus flower, which can clean itself in the rain.

The light is an important aspect of well-being in our homes, and the affect of daylight on home is invaluable. Make sure that you pull open your curtains and blinds. Do not try to block the windows; this has a tendency to create a bad atmosphere.

Growth helps us create life. Take good care of anything living. Fish that are not given enough food and clean water, and flowers in need of attention, speak of a lack of caring for life.

In that case, it is better to be without. To take care of flowers is a way of developing care for yourself and others.

In order to create a home with a nice atmosphere, space is important. Create space between furniture by not setting them too close to each other, and feel free to bind them together through floor rugs. Rugs have an important function in creating harmony. Choose large rugs and let them slip under your sofa. When you buy a rug, make sure that it is not impregnated with toxic substances.

Nostalgia is a dear wabi-sabi subject. Things that are connected to people you may have cared about, things that make your heart warmer, pictures and objects that speak to you directly—all of these things are important in creating a comfortable home.

Design

People throw away what they could have by insisting on perfection, which they cannot have, and looking for it where they will never find it

EDITH SCHAEFFER

The term wabi-sabi design is now commonly used. Nature and timeless beauty is the basis. It is about design with care; it is a way of living closely and intimately with materials, colors, and shapes.

It is often said that we humans shouldn't be so materialistic, but maybe that it exactly what we need to be, but in a new way—a way where we tenderly value our things and view them in a deeper way. Surely the closeness to the things around us can create an inner well-being and enjoyment.

It is important from a design perspective to place the functionality before the decoration. A chair should first and foremost be comfortable; it should be lasting and easy to use. Not until these things are in place can you consider how it looks.

Wabi sabi brings design in to a fascinating world. A pottery maker needs to experience the clay as a living creature in order to really use it to create beauty. When a designer lives with the material, genuine craftsmanship follows. A simplicity rests over wabi sabi; there is a minimum of details. There are no set forms—wabi sabi withstands all trends.

The design is pretty raw and unrefined, which is what makes it so breathtaking. It is often uneven, tarnished, organic, and a little random. You should be able to feel time in the material to achieve the real feeling of wabi sabi. It is when we wear things lovingly that the real feeling arises.

You won't often find strong and bright colors in wabi sabi; the colors are often softer and closer to nature. It advocates space, but not bright light.

You will rarely find perfect symmetry in wabi sabi; the teachings of nature are behind this. There is no absolute symmetry in nature, unless there is a reason there should be symmetry. If you want to work with decorating and design, a sense of the rough symmetry is important.

As opposed to feng shui, wabi sabi contains very little symbolism. It is life, nature, and the timeless beauty that leads the way. In other words, we enjoy more here and now than dream about the future.

Japanese art and design can sometimes seem strict and almost brutal in its shape, but a beauty still rests over it. What one strives for is life; the unpolished life away from all illusions of "happiness." Personally, I might not choose the strict Zen-Buddhist design that you often see in the context of wabi sabi. And it is important to note that you should first and foremost choose things that make you feel well and look beautiful to you. Tastes vary, but timeless beauty lasts.

One of the things I love more than anything in wabi-sabi design is the term *li*. Li is a soft sweeping stroke, like a careful breath. It is all over nature: You can see li as a soft line on the sky or in a pile of snow where the wind has given the snow soft lines. Li is found on the human body; for instance the neck and bottom—areas that have always fascinated artists. The ability to create a li-line is not obvious, but it is often apparent when we are in touch with the wisdom and love in us; it is about a feeling of wanting to move in a different way.

What one seeks in wabi-sabi design

- Timeless beauty.
- Function before decoration.
- Rough organic shapes.
- No obvious design
- Often mellow, darker colors.
- Complexity in colors and materials.
- Easy to use.
- The natural.
- What feel interesting and fascinating.
- Li-shapes.

The garden

Adopt the pace of nature; her secret is patience

RALPH WALDO EMERSON

In the context of gardens, you can view wabi sabi in two ways. One way is the Japanese cultural way, where the Zen Buddhism is a large influence; there rules a harsh and crude silence. It is meditational, has few things—a garden space that feels sacred. The other way is to take the garden as it is and feel content with it; a garden where you rest and follow the changing of seasons and maybe even grow something edible. Always allow your garden to take time, and remember that it will never be perfect; never finished. Enjoy it as it is.

WATER

Water is important in all gardens; it creates life and movement. Water has a quite easily graspable symbolism—it is about the flow of life and both inner and outer riches. Gratitude and order often follow in the water's path. Make sure that the water flows and doesn't stand still, and that it is clean. You will often see dripping water in wabi-sabi gardens—it encourages silence and contemplation.

LI

Li is the sweeping movement that is so important to Japanese philosophy (although the strict Zen-Buddhist shape may be quite square). Let ladders, edges, and other shapes in your garden have a carefully waved line. Use a water hose when you create pathways and thresholds, this way you can picture how it will turn out. Move around it and look at it from multiple angles before you complete the work.

Many cultures use various sacred geometric shapes. The golden section is one of them; an incredibly harmonic proportion (see page 133). If you, for instance, want to make a threshold, you only need to know the measure of the short end or the long end to create the golden section. If the short side, for instance, is 13 feet, you multiply this by 1.618—and you see that the long side should be 21 feet. If you know the length of the longest side you divide that measurement by 1.618 (21/1.618=13).

There are many other exciting geometric shapes you can use, such as the circle. You can also toy with the platonic bodies, which are the building bricks of the universe, or why not use a pentagon for a rim? Sacred geometry is a wonderful world to visit, where precision is vital and the result is magic.

MYSTICISM AND MAGIC

Create mysticism in your garden with exciting openings and unexpected solutions. You can even use symbolism to create magic, even if one traditionally is quite careful with symbolism in wabi sabi. But anything that provides enjoyment, peace of mind, happiness, reverence, silence, and tenderness is valuable.

BALANCE AND HARMONY

Make it simple and enjoy the timeless beauty that nature gives a garden. Balance and harmony is most often created when we compose in contrasts: Set light against dark; sharper leaves with softer leaves; stone with water; straight lines with soft lines; tall growths with shorter ones. Creating a timelessly beautiful garden may also mean not blending too many different growths.

If you wish to step further into wabi sabi and Japanese culture, you should create a Zen garden. The garden builds upon extreme silence and raw beauty, so think of materials like stone and metals. Use water, white colors; avoid excess and decorations. Simple, tasteful and unrefined, as simple as that. Bonsai trees belong in Zen

---

Wabi sabi design in the garden

- Careful and meticulous balance (look at nature).
- Silence and simplicity, no excess.
- No set forms.
- No unity.
- Natural, not forced.
- Lots of space.
- A minimum of details.
- Unrefined/raw.
- Local materials or recycled.
- Not sensitive to trends.
- Naturally frayed.
- Uneven and asymmetrical.
- Variated.
- Random.
- None or very little symbolism.
- Shapes that follow the nature of the material.

gardens, and creating bonsai trees is a science in itself. Remember to work with the plant so that you do not violate it.

THE BACKGROUND OF THE GARDEN

Does your garden have a history? Is there a way that you can honor this history? Personally, I have allowed old growths that have been in our garden from before I showed up, remain as part of the house and area's history. I also know that the first owner of the house loved yew tress, so I have left these as well as a memory of the family that built the house. Planting trees for future generations is a symbolic wabi-sabi action.

THE ENTRANCE

Every garden is affected by how the entrance looks. Even if you don't create a grand feng-shui entrance with lighting, symbols, and other impressive elements, you should think of reverence, carefulness, and for it to be welcoming. Keep the entrance clean, quiet, and beautiful. The entrance says a lot about the person living there. Make sure that you greet yourself into your garden in a worthy manner.

THE COMPOST

Few things are as fantastic as witnessing how nature makes fresh, powerful dirt out of old life. Remember to take care of your compost—enjoy it and situate it so that it is accessible but a little hidden. I often think of the human life processes as a compost. Where in the body is your compost? I place mine in the uterus and pull my pain, sorrow, and despair down there. There everything is composted to new seeds of wisdom and strength. It rarely serves you well to keep your compost in your head!

THE RAKE

Meditation and afterthought are wabi-sabi words. When wabi sabi was born in Japan, the rake and the broom were important elements. In wabi sabi you rarely sit still, but rather you rest in what is and what you create. Few things are as calming as raking or sweeping. One would often rake a pattern in pebbles as a sign that one in reverence and silence created something. If you have a pebbled path in your garden—get a rake!

THE STONES

Stone silences and calms us. To use a focus stone in the garden may mean placing a special stone at the end of a path or by a sitting area/contemplation spot.

"Flokus" is a newer word which is about flow and focus at the same time; this is where you get if you rest in yourself and in all that is going on while at the same time being aware of where you are going.

FOLLOW THE RHYTHM

Praise the rhythm of the seasons in your garden and in life. Small, simple ceremonies brighten the existence and show that we care about all that is happening. We can greet spring through a fire, and fall through quietly gathering and arranging fall growths. The thought of pace creates the wonderful wabi-sabi space, the sense that nothing lasts forever. We take too much for granted, and we're bewildered when they disappear. In the garden, we can follow the cycle of life and witness how nothing disappears forever.

A GARDEN FOR YOUR HEALTH

The drug industry earns enormous sums of money these days. If we would rather use nature and our gardens more, I am convinced that we would be able to lower the consumption of drugs considerably while also creating better health and higher life quality.

Close contact with nature has the following effect on the human body:

- The skeleton is strengthened and osteoporosis is prevented.
- Muscles get stronger and movement is maintained.
- Prevents obesity.
- Sleep quality is bettered.
- Prevents anxiety and depression.
- Resistance to infections grow stronger.
- Tolerance for stress is heightened.
- Prevents acute heart conditions.
- Encourages social life and prevents solitude.
- Lowers pulse and blood pressure.
- Can prove a positive affect on brain activity.
- Pain relief occurs

(Source: Rikard Küller and Marianne Küller, Stadens grönska, äldres utevistelse och hälsa. National series for Building Research, 1994)

❀

Timeless beauty

The hours when the mind is absorbed by beauty are the only hours when we really live.

RICHARD JEFFERIES

Timeless beauty may be said to be a signature of wabi sabi. The term describes how you create a good life. Where it is beautiful, good things happen, and where it is not beautiful, bad things happen.

Very few things can heal a human soul as quickly as beauty. It is almost like the soul feeds on beauty. We know this instinctively, but we rarely use this knowledge. We have spent close to a century on research within psychology and all of the things that concern human well-being but this research has never focused on the healing powers of beauty. Humans become unhappy in ugly environments; the beauty gives us dignity and hope.

And what is beautiful? Is beauty not in the eye of the beholder? People repeatedly ask this question, and wabi sabi stands for what we call timeless beauty. In order to describe this beauty, we have to connect it with nature. Timeless beauty is the beauty that always remains, the beauty that was appreciated 1,000 years ago and that will still be here in 500 more years. We find it in nature and where humans are in contact with their hearts and souls. It is pure, and it is innocent. Sometimes it can be heartbreakingly stunning. Heartbreaking beauty is created when we are in contact with the core of wabi sabi: That everything in life is temporary.

You cannot measure beauty in material terms; it is an experience of how much you are in contact with your inner self and the truth that life stands for.

A couple of years back a scientist wanted to prove that my theories around beauty and feng shui were wrong. He heat-photographed a furnished room; later he threw all of the furniture down to the floor and did another heat-photo. He then exclaimed: "There, you see—the energy in the room is exactly the same!"

I didn't know whether to laugh or cry. To measure balance, harmony, beauty, or love is impossible. It is like trying to measure the deep of love with a sonar and proclaim that love doesn't exist since the instrument doesn't react. These will most likely always remain immeasurable and indefinable grandeurs.

The hunger and longing for beauty is extremely great these days. Industrialism threw craftsmanship aside; and science, Darwinism, and modernism threw the timeless beauty aside and proclaimed that everything could be measured and explained—that those who were best equipped for survival would survive, and that straight lines, empty surfaces, function, and squared shapes should go before other ways of expression. Today we have reached a breaking point where beauty is on its way back. An increasing amount of people search for the inner values that the timeless beauty stands for.

God has been a source of beauty in all religions, no matter how you perceive it. The timeless beauty is proof of the existence of a higher power.

When a person creates something with her hands, she will automatically create something beautiful (as long one does not carry deeper damage on the inside). To create beauty gives enjoyment. Beauty is about being able to see, listen, feel, and be in contact with nature and one's own soul.

We have many timelessly beautiful creations that will always impress most of humanity. Part of these are the music of Mozart and The Beatles; the art of Leonardo da Vinci and Monet; buildings like the Parthenon temple in Athens and the cathedral in Chartres. It is time to reclaim beauty, even if it doesn't have to be as perfect as these works. Wabi sabi is modest and protects the small beauty, the beauty that exists everywhere—in our palms, in the bark of a tree, on a leaf, in the meeting between two people where they're hearts are open and vulnerable. I believe, that many of the depressions of today is a result of the lack of listening, looking, and feeling.

When we create beauty, sensuality and enjoyment always follows. Few things are more helpful in climbing out of depression and hard times than creativity. Our hands want to create beauty; there is no longing in us to create things that are ugly. The ugliness is often about a person's longing after a manifestation, maybe because of a wounded inner. We have seen architects and decorators revel in their desire to create monuments of themselves. But beauty and the deep gifts are about surrendering to the creational power of art and nature's wisdom.

The spokesperson and writer Henrik Fexeus once did an experiment: He was arranging a lecture where half of the audience had to wait in advance in a homey room with table cloths, flowers, candles, and a fruit bowl, while the other group had to wait on a concrete culvert with worn furniture and with a thermos filled with lukewarm coffee that they drank from plastic cups. When the lecture was over, he looked at the evaluation of him as a lecturer. The people that had waited in the homey room all gave him good scores, whereas the ones that had been in the ugly room gave him negative criticism (the audience was, of course, ignorant of the project).

What does this teach us? Well, that humans that reside in wonderful and carefully decorated rooms are more positive. Why is it then that we allow so many ugly official spaces, like schools and hospitals? As a result of studies, we now know that patients regain their health more quickly when they have access to a window and a view of nature.

One of the reasons why we've created so much ugly design throughout the years is the fact that the people behind the architecture in their turn have made the design at a desk with a computer, without really taking in the place in question. They simply made the design far from reality. We now need to recreate a sense of proportion; for instance when it comes to situate a window harmoniously. This was well known in older architecture, but the knowledge seems to have been forgotten in much of newer architecture.

Within wabi sabi one often points out that everything is not as it seems. The following story is proof of just that:

> Washington D.C., a metro station on a cold morning in January 2007.
> A man with a violin plays Bach for one hour. During this hour about 2,000 people walk past.
> After three minutes a middle-aged man notices the musician and slows his walk. He stops for a few seconds and then later continues on his way.
> After four minutes the violinist receives his first dollar; a woman throws the coin in his hat without stopping.
> After about six minutes a younger man stops and listens for a while but soon glances at his watch and moves on.
> After 10 minutes a child of about 10 stops, but his mother pulls him with her. (Multiple children stopped, but were without fail dragged on by their parents.)
> After 45 minutes, only 6 people stopped to listen for a short while. Around 20 people have thrown money in his hat, most without slowing down. The violinist gathers $32 altogether.
> After one hour the musician stops playing and it goes quiet. Nobody notices that he stops and nobody claps.

The musician that was playing was Joshua Bell, one of the world's foremost violinists. He played some of Bach's most demanding pieces, on a violin worth $3.5 million.

Two days before, Joshua Bell had performed at sold-out shows in Boston. The tickets went for an average of $100.

This is a true story. Joshua Bell's incognito performance at the metro station was organized by *The Washington Post,* as part of a sociological experiment about perception, taste, and human priorities.

One wonders: Do we even notice the beauty in our everyday environment at an inconvenient time? Do we recognize talent in an unsuspected environment? How many of us goes to concerts and pay good money for something we do not have the sense to appreciate?

A last note in the whirlwind of thoughts: If we do not choose to stop when one of the world's best musicians plays some of the world's most beautiful pieces on one of the world's most beautiful instruments— what and how much else are we missing without even realizing it?

The sacred geometry

Geometry is a mathematical appreciation of how various parts of something are related to one another. The term "sacred geometry" is about entering the deep and mirroring what one would say has timeless beauty. When you reach an accuracy in geometry, a communication is created in the human inner self that leads to peace of mind. We instinctively feel that it is right and it gives us peace; we experience beauty, balance, and harmony inside and we come in contact with a form of higher consciousness. The human gets the chance to heal when she is surrounded by harmonic proportions.

One example of sacred geometry is the golden section. There we see the proportions and a heavenly image, where the measurements are magnificently calculated mathematically in order to recreate the creation of God in a geometric shape.

I have learned to feel my body when a window or a door is proportionally created and has a sacred geometry. I can simply feel when the lines are right. You do not have to be particularly interested to have this intuitive feeling or to exercise it. I have seen it in a variety of real craftsmen that cannot say why the line or object should be just where they placed it, they just know that it feels right!

You can find sacred geometry everywhere; look at your own body and its proportions. If you want to learn more about the phenomenon of our bodies, Leonardo Da Vinci's famous drawing of the Vitruvian Man is worth a look. Da Vinci was convinced that the human body represents the perfect relationship between soulfulness and matter, something that is mirrored in its proportions.

You find the sacred geometry in nature. You may describe the spiral snail shape in exact mathematical terms with Fibonacci's famous number series from the 1200s (the series starts: 0, 1, 1, 2, 3, 5, 8, 13, 21, 34). Fibonacci's number series is connected to the golden section in an exciting way. If you divide a given number with the previous, you get closer to the golden section the higher the numbers get.

You can find the golden section in your wallet: Credit cards often have this shape. As does, for instance, the Swedish flag.

If we go far back in time, the sacred geometry was incredibly important. The oldest known document with exact geometric instructions is a Hindu manuscript with plans for building temples. Even in Egypt and the old Babylon, we have found traces of geometry from around 3000 B.C. Sacred places like Stonehenge in England and the most famous pyramids in Gaza are built on very meticulous mathematical analyses. Some of these analyses are so sophisticated that the mathematicians of today would have trouble understanding them.

The old Greeks perceived geometry as the highest of all sciences and they developed it further. Plato (427–347 B.C.) wrote over the entrance of his famous school: "Let None But Geometers Enter Here." Plato was not a mathematician, but his ideas of mathematics have been of great influence. He had three guidelines in his own work: "It should be good, it should be true, and it should be beautiful." These have become words to live by for me personally as well.

If all people were to follow the motto that we should be good, true, and beautiful—what an exciting world we would see! In the future, old knowledge will be brought out and age once more: We are simply too wise to move on in some ways.

Sensuality is one of the feminine gifts, and most likely women react more to ugly surroundings than men. The feminine power deepens and refines beautiful colors, shapes, music, and art, so freeze in beauty, sensuality, and transcendence! Wabi sabi wants her daughters to enjoy their existence, and in turn women that enjoy give a huge gift to the masculine power.

Beauty gives the soul dignity and respect. Where it is beautiful, we will create life; there we will nurture life—this is where we need to go to save the world from stupidity.

Food

Wabi sabi is the opposite of "too much," and when we approach the subject of food, this has really reached breathtaking proportions. Never has so much food been divided so unevenly across the world—obesity and hunger exists together in a unfathomable and devastating imbalance. In a small part of the world, large quantities of food are thrown out, while there is a lack of food in most places. How did it go so wrong?

Surely there are many answers to this question, but one thing is certain: We have to start considering how we are thinking. Are we thinking with our brain, sense, logic, or heart?

Worldwatch institute presented a six-year plan where they estimated the cost of protecting fertile ground, balancing woods, decreasing the growth of our population, writing off the debts of the third world, utilizing energy better, and developing sustainable energy sources—in other words saving the world. This would 730 billion. This may sound like a lot, but if we put it up against the fact that we yearly spend 1,000 billion kroners on the weapons industry, the choice seems easy. It is sometimes said that the road between the brain and heart is the world's longest distance, but it is about time that we close up this gap.

A while back I met a man that worked in the health industry and was a real food guru. He knew all there was to know about food and what it contains, how it should be prepared and everything else. He wouldn't eat this and he wouldn't eat that, and absolutely not that . . .

It had been a while since I had seen such a stressed, skinny, and haggard person in the search for the good life. The worst part was that I could see myself in the hunt for the right and the good. Ultimately the hunt may be so focused and tiring that it turns into something unhealthy before we even realize what happened.

We know so much about food these days, and there are so many "good" diets to choose from. Of course there are good aspects in this, but from a wabi sabi perspective there is a voice saying: "Maybe you should start by sitting down when you eat . . ."

There are studies made on children where they've been given something similar to a huge smorgasbord. The study was performed to see what children would eat if they were free to choose. What they found was that they ate the simple things, they did not over eat, and they didn't blend the flavors together. In our eyes, their plates may have looked quite pathetic. The study revealed that over the course of a few weeks, their more-than-modest diet had provided them with a good nutritional intake.

What can we learn from this? Maybe that we do not need to make food into such a big deal, but rather eat simpler, purer, and more naturally, and listen to our bodies instead of all of the dieting advice.

Wabi sabi stands for eating as simple and respectfully as possible. When we do this, it becomes natural to take it one step further and start eating local food and as organically as possible. We should eat in an environment that provides calm and peace, and the possibility of afterthought and gratitude over the gift food really is.

Food is not a human right, it is a gift. It is not until we are without food what we realize the depth of this gift.

It is important to exercise our ability to see things as a gift. When I stayed at a friends house a while back and we were eating breakfast in the morning we only had toast and milk. This is not something I would normally choose for breakfast, and if it were not for my meeting with wabi sabi, there is a large chance that I would be complaining inside. Instead, I now chose to see the breakfast as a gift, and to be honest, I enjoyed it!

I have never given my body a fasting experience—something that is common in wabi sabi—but I have at times decreased the outer stimulation in my life to allow my body rest. I perceive these periods of time as longer. I can uncontrollably enjoy a simple soup by myself at the table, or a cup of tea out on the porch. There are still moments when I fly into the stress rollercoaster and eat in my car or run to a meeting without eating at all, but it hurts the body and soul after a while. My meeting with wabi sabi has changed my attitude. I can't imagine ever living a life constantly out of breath ever again.

If you want to do a wabi-sabi fast, you need to give your body a lot of rest during that time, eat simply, and slowly decrease your intake. The most important element in a fast is rest for the body and soul, and that it is a time for reflection and admiration of life. If possible, spend your fasting period in a calm place, without TV, telephone, and so on. The quiet is important for the possibility of self-reflection.

Wabi sabi does not merely call food good or bad; various kinds of food affects your specific body in various ways. It is not always what you eat that matters, but how you eat it. It is actually better to sit at McDonald's and enjoy your meal than sitting at home eating a salad while counting calories with the anxiety hovering over you.

My first fitness instructor always said: "Whatever you do, do it with pleasure. And no matter what you drink or eat, enjoy it. It is the anxiety that hurts us the most." I have tried this, and I can drink a glass of Coca-Cola and really enjoy it, but my body reacts after one glass, and the enjoyment is over. If you're a smoker, you can enjoy the cigarettes as long as you are smoking, but you will reach a point where the body doesn't enjoy it anymore, and it is easier to quit at this time than when you try to force your body to make a decision, and you create an angst-filled situation for every blow you take.

There are certain foodstuffs that deserve mentioning, and those are tea, onion, eggs, and bread.

The tea ceremonies in Japan are well-known. They are sometimes called—just like wabi sabi—the religion of beauty. Traditionally, tea would be consumed in special rooms that were simply and sparingly decorated, according to the Zen-Buddhist pattern. The cups of tea are important objects, and they often have a rustic and beautiful design.

When I first seriously entered wabi sabi, I practiced drinking tea and learned to embrace the ritual in itself. Today it is one of the gifts I enjoy most in life. It is the silence and afterthought that comes with drinking tea that has touched me. My nine-year-old daughter loves the simple ritual of sitting quietly (most times) and in the dark by the kitchen table with just one lit candle and drinking our tea. It is a holy moment for the two of us.

I generally love to eat in quiet, this way I can really taste the food and feel how much I enjoy eating. For many, a quiet meal is far from the reality of the day, and in those cases it might be more important to gather the whole family around the table for a meal.

Onions and eggs are two other raw materials that make the wabi-sabi heart beat a little faster. The onion is symbolically important, with its layers upon layers. It reminds us of people and perceptions of life, where there are always multiple layers. If there's damage of some sort somewhere on the onion, you can always peel and find a layer further down that is healthy.

The egg is the symbol of female reproduction and is viewed as the finest of all gifts of nature that provides nurture. When you view the egg this way, it gives the food an extra dimension.

Bread is holy in all cultures and should have a greater focus today. To eat bread that's never been touched by hands may not feel as holy, and maybe the baking of bread will receive its renaissance with the growing interest in wabi sabi.

In a reportage of how we will live in 2019, the future strategist and ethnologist Ida Hult says that we will take a greater responsibility in how we contribute to a better world. This will also include that we will buy and live with quality, both when it comes to food and things. Throwing out food and eating strawberries that have been flown in from southern countries will be an ethical decision. She says: "We are going to want to share, not only our money, but also our emotions. We will be tired of greed and commerce, and rather we will want quality in products and relationships. Giving is already larger than taking, but the next step is sharing . . ."

The trend analyst Lennart Wallander says that, in the year 2019, the conscious diner will be cooking for the future. We are already tired of preservatives, and we realize that we are affecting millions through what we eat. He says: "In 2019, it will be standard, a given, that we ask for locally produced foods and follow the Northern food season." He also states that the most ambitious of us will start growing our own vegetables, both in the wild and in our gardens in the city.

An interesting phenomenon that has emerged in England especially is that people who own gardens, but have no interesting in cultivating food, will lend their gardens to the ones with an interest but no access to fertile ground. This can become an invaluable win-win solution, where in exchange for the ground, you may receive some of the crop.

The wabi-sabi kitchen

You should decorate your kitchen in a way that allows you to feel comfortable there; that is the most important. It should feel good to cook in the kitchen, and it should feel wonderful and calming to sit there and eat. Combining wabi sabi with feng shui, which is the Chinese teaching of how you decorate to allow your surroundings to support you, is a very good basis. (See my previous books, *Feng Shui for Swedish Homes,* and *Living with Feng Shui.)*

What would inspire you where you cook? Nice cookbooks, beautiful candles, colorful vegetables, the smell of herbs? Think with your heart and let your fantasy roam free. At home, we've built a kitchen island so that we can stand and observe our home while we cook, and at the same time stay in contact with out children. We prioritized a nice oven, good knifes, and a robust cutting block.

In a wabi-sabi kitchen, you will look at the utilities and pots more closely. It doesn't have to be new things—the allure of wabi sabi is that the slightly worn may still be used. To me, it is special to take out my grandmother's old dough bowls and ladles that I know she used; they remind me of my childhood, which I associate with her warmth and her fantastic food.

Rustic objects belong in the wabi-sabi kitchen—a simple design and preferably with mainly earth elements; that is to say, earth colors. The floor with wide floorboards, the wood-burning stove, and the decor awe many of the people who see my kitchen. What very few people know is that I found the floor, stove, and décor myself, and paid very little for them. Wabi sabi has no need for expensive things—unless there is a good reason for it.

A wabi-sabi kitchen is free from messiness—but doesn't mean that there can't be creative chaos! However, stagnated chaos should be avoided, where the messiness is permanent, and many things are never used.

Start off by removing everything in the kitchen that you do not like or use. It may be time to look through old cookbooks—you can give these away, or you might find something you like in them so that you can start using them.

Avoid the cold and sharp in the kitchen—although knifes should of course be sharp!—and strengthen everything that creates community and cooking joy. I think that many of the kitchens of tomorrow will have an open fireplace; until then, we might have to settle for lit candles. A candle designer once taught me that if you keep tall candles on the dinner table, everyone sitting around it will get a small glimmer of light in their eyes, and the small glimmer awakens a longing in us to know each other better . . .

Cooking can be a nice way of resurrecting the joy of food. Our family is part of a food team that meets one Friday of every month. Cooking together is so much more stimulating! Music is another element that may bring joy to cooking; it is simply more fun to cook with music.

When I bring the food out I always say thank you, either out loud or to myself. If I am preparing meat, I give a silent thank you to the animal that gave its life for us. To show appreciation and gratitude for the ingredients is part of a life attitude.

Personally I eat game, but many devoted wabi sabi practitioners do not eat meat. It is not the thought of killing that is the main reason, but rather how the meat industry of today functions. Life and death are of equal value in wabi sabi; everything is an eternal circular movement, without beginning and without end.

Right living is no longer only the fulfillment of an ethical or religious demand. For the first time in history the physical survival of the human race depends on a radical change of the human heart.

ERICH FROMM, FROM *TO HAVE OR TO BE?*

The good work life

Contentment is natural wealth, luxury is artificial poverty.

SOCRATES

Work is a part of our existence that usually holds a large place. How does the good work life look? What do I have the right to expect from work? Is it a gift that I have work at all?

Wabi sabi has given my work life a real shake. I started working way too early and way too hard. When I, as a fourteen-year-old, was faced with the fact that I might have to manage on my own, I got scared. I basically forgot about school and threw myself into a work hunt. I found a part-time position at both a bakery and a gas station. It felt good to know that I would be able to manage economically if the worst were to happen. School, of course, became a nightmare. I struggled through a high school education with a concentration in economics, but I had so much additional work that I couldn't spend time on my studies.

When I first met wabi sabi, work had been in my blood for so long that the meeting became sort of a detox. I had previously been afraid of having time off and being unproductive, but now I realized that what I had been doing had made me miss so much of life. I had not left any room for play, enjoyment, and rest.

It was difficult to build this new view on work and rest. But I am still grateful for what my previous experiences have given me. It has made me into a person who knows what she wants, knows what she should do, and makes sure that she does it. I still have trouble accepting help from someone or something; I am so used to managing on my own. This has given me an incredible drive, and I still use this power today in a humbler and healthier way.

My own experiences have made me wonder about how we act when it comes to our children and youth. Giving them all that they want may become a devastating lesson for them, since they do not learn to work for the thing they want. The thought of a generation with people who just sit around and wait scares me.

Wabi sabi gives us the insight that we can make our own lives. To me, work is a way of serving life; it is a gift I want to convey to others. Today, my work is no longer driven by fear, but by caring. Every day I ask that life will use me in the best possible way.

If we look around us in the world, we can recognize a large collective fear. For many people, questions such as "What if I lose my job?", "What if I am no longer needed?", and "What if my workplace goes bankrupt?" follow them everyday.

The writer and yoga teacher Tomas Frankell once said: "There is no unemployment for the soul." I agree. There will always be a place for human contribution. This is a calming comfort. Your intuition and your ability to rest and listen to the right answers will lead you in the right direction. If there's courage and will, life will always present solutions, but we have to tone down the surrounding noise to hear the wisdom inside us. When weights of worry and fear wash over us, we need to be practiced in resting and just going with the flow. It will pass.

Wabi sabi also teaches us that no work is perfect, no work lasts forever, and no work will ever be finished. If we can learn to live with these facts and do the best we can, the soul may find enjoyment. And that is the goal of wabi sabi.

All people have value, and all people can contribute to the whole in one way or another. Even if I lie paralyzed in my bed, I can open my heart and give my love to the children of the world. This gives life meaning. I once heard about a woman who thought her life was so meaningless that she was going to end it. Her savior was a lone cat that came to her home. She decided to make sure that the cat had a worthy life. This gave her the will to live back and the ability to rebuild it.

We can create the good work life with wabi sabi. In order to do this, we need to go back to the cornerstones of the subject: quiet, flow, enjoyment, respect, kindness, generosity, nature as wisdom, creativity, passion, cooperation good relationships. Work life will get a real boost with the development of these qualities. No matter where you are and what you do, you can always strive for these qualities. You can create a good work life, but we have to start with ourselves.

Feminine principles in the work life include:

- Creating a harmonic wholeness.
- Listening to your heart and following its conviction.
- Being open to new and unknown paths.
- Shielding diversity and originality.
- Maintaining a sense of wonder.
- Respecting the unique expression of every individual.
- Working in a way that cares for future generations.
- Trusting the institution first, and the intellect second.
- Creating corporation and win-win situations.
- Maintaining balance with nature in everything; giving and receiving.
- Running ecologically long-term and sustainable businesses and organizations.
- Not compromising our inner truth.

I have always valued cooperation and good business relations. I think this explains many of my work processes. I never think in terms of the competitor, but rather "if as many as possible win, the world will be more fun to live in."

In wabi sabi, you never just think of yourself. You always have to think of what you create in a larger and wider perspective. If you compete—how will the loser feel if you win? What do the emotions of that person create in the rest of the world? How will that person act as a parent? How do his/her children feel about the situation?

Many would answer: "That's not my problem", but in wabi sabi, it is our problem. Everything we do and everything we help create is our responsibility. Whether it concerns your children or mine doesn't matter.

What does competition and rivalry provide in the long run? Does it create peace of mind, respect, cooperation, and a worthy life? Wabi sabi knows that nothing lasts forever. Only the things you are willing to give to others have a constant worth. Give while you can, because sooner or later it will be taken from you by age, health, and other circumstances.

Generosity and honor are leading words in wabi sabi. And it is true what the old wisdom says: The more you give to others, the more you will receive in return. When I, for instance, buy services from a teacher, I sometimes see that they are uncomfortable with asking to be paid. But it doesn't give me joy to buy their services on the cheap. It is noble to pay (if I can), so that people can make a living.

Generosity is the flow of life. If I hold the flow back in order to gain other things, I suffocate the flow in myself. I am grateful that I early on stumbled upon a book called *Moneylove* by Jerry Gillies. It taught me the magic of how money, generosity, and flow works.

There is a study that shows that when people earn more than $30,000 (200,000 kroners) each year, the equal sign between money and joy disappears. Of course we may be happy when we earn more money, but we will still have 48 problems (see page 74)—and with money, you'll find other kinds of problems.

When I experienced successes with books a few years back and earned a significant amount more than I had done previously in my life, one of my biggest problems became how people perceived it and how they reacted. I lost some "old friends" when I succeeded and I met jealousy for the first time in my life; I also gained many "new friends." But many of them turned out to be after other things than what I, in my naivety, had imagined.

If you really want to experience enjoyment over your work, you should keep the threshold on a normal level. Take one step at a time and let the heart lead you. Be generous, create a network, and get a partner. Take moments or days where you allow the silence to rule so the right decisions may be made.

Longer workweeks and overtime are things wabi sabi warns about. The more you work, the more you get done, people say. Is it not rather true that the more rested, focused, and sharp you are, the more you get done? There are so many tired, drowsy, and annoyed people in the world today, who do not perform as they could. We need rest and rejuvenation to complete the work efficiently. The hunt for expansion and addition at any price erodes the soul of our work life.

For something to last long-term we have to sow the seeds, water, give nutrition, be patient, and wait . . . Imagine a flower that's been cultivated artificially: It has one goal—to blossom for as long as possible and be beautiful for as long as possible. These hard-driven growths are beautiful, they blossom, but they don't keep for many years. The question we ask ourselves is: Will we last for many years?

It is like the tale of the farmer who asks God to be able to control the weather so that his crops turn out well. He knows exactly how much rain is needed, how much sun there should be, how many insects are best. He is allowed to play God for a couple of years, and his crop grows and becomes fantastic. But after a few years, the plants start to wither. They get weaker and weaker, despite the fact that they get the exact amount of water and light that they need. They have simply gotten so spoiled that they've lost their original viability.

This is what wabi sabi tries to teach us about difficulties. They should harden us and make us vital. If we only got what we wanted, we would grow weak.

Wabi sabi appreciates originality over copies. Are we, and what we work with, originals or a mass-produced copy? All copies dilute the soul of the world. We should not peek at each other and steal ideas. We should be inspired and cultivate our own concepts that support the world's future. There are lots of exciting concepts to be inspired by.

Seek people and ideas, take part in innovative solutions, and seek the likeminded. The power is never as strong as when it is pulled by people who are walking in the same direction. The worst thing that can happen at a workplace is that everyone pulls in different directions, and nobody knows the guidelines. The basis for growth in the workplace is that people know where they are going, how to get there, and that the look forward to the journey. The goal is never the most important in wabi sabi—the journey is the focus.

Wabi sabi asks us to see things as they are and not in any other way. I have a work colleague who does not share my views, and I can tell that I would really like her to—everything would be so much simpler that way. But when she goes against me, I have to find a way to deal with that. Either walk away or respect her views as they are. And life is so much easier if we do the latter. It would be disturbing if everyone thought and acted the same after all. We would be a large pile of copies of ourselves. Differences are valuable!

Do you often compare things? This is a dangerous trap that we should watch out for. For instance, do you know if you always buy things because you really want it, or because you compare yourself to others?

Find your own way of relating to things—try to let go of trends, fashions, and group pressure. Find your unique style and see if you can develop it work-wise.

I always know that I am on the wrong track when I start thinking in the line of trends and what would make the most money. The gift and flow comes from the passion for creating what we think is fun, and not until after can one start thinking of how to make it profitable. If the money and profitability comes first, that business side will be on rocky ground.

Scientists believe that in the future we will work in a different way than we do today and hopefully for less hours, which would mean that more people could work. Many of the monotonous jobs will disappear. It will be harder for traditional businesses to find passionate people to hire; most people will embrace their freedom. Large changes will come, which are vital in order for us, and the planet, to be well.

Tina Brown, former editor of the magazine *Vanity Fair,* coined the term "gigonomics." This is based in the word "gig" and it states that, in the future, people will work with a variety of things at the same time in their work life—a little copywriting, a little article writing, some office work, and so on. This will involve more network-building, and people will be able to tailor their own careers with the help of their personal goals and evaluations. This provides options and opens a space for originality, which wabi sabi encourages.

I think the intensive time we now live in teaches us a few important things, and that is discernment and the art of answering the large questions in life.

- What is important?
- What do I want?
- How do my choices affect me?
- Which traces do I leave behind on the planet?
- Am I an original or a copy?
- Who/what controls my life?
- What is the most loving thing I can do right now?

Vision and focus occur in a rested mind when one has learned the ability to set boundaries in life. We live in a world where so many things can grab us and pull us away. If it's not the phone, it is the internet or some other impulse that feeds our minds. Rest and separation is fundamental for a mind in harmony. We can be afraid to ask the big questions, but remember that the answers will always come in moderate amounts. It's incredibly wonderful when it is done, and you know that you've given the body what it needs.

Walking in wabi sabi

The following key words are clues to a life in wabi sabi.

Devotion: Open your heart, dare to enter the deep, no matter what happens.

Give life and nurture: Always look for the things that give nurture and create life.

Unconditional love: Love without expectations, even if it is hard.

Grace, mercy: Do not judge or criticize.

Tenderness, humility: Observe lovingly, be caring with yourself and others.

Timeless beauty: Create and protect the things that have lasting beauty.

Sensuousness: Move carefully, experience your senses.

Homecoming: Rest in yourself.

Choose love first: Ask yourself what love would choose.

Healing: Open your heart even when it is tough.

Quiet spirituality: Prayer, rest, quiet, silence, self-reflection.

Integrity: Stand up for what you believe in.

Strength and courage: Challenge yourself even if you are scared.

Vulnerability: Dare to be vulnerable and naked before yourself and others.

Independence and individuality: Clear up unhealthy dependence.

Limitlessness: See large, see white, see endless, live deep.

Setting boundaries: Mark boundaries where it is needed—soft, but firm and clear.

Sexuality: Play, affirm, discover.

Sensuality: Rest, move slowly, enjoy.

Enjoyment: Experience through all the senses.

Wild natural force: Affirm life through dancing, singing, playing, laughing, and crying.

Death and rebirth: Accept the cycles of life, accept change.

Deep ecstasy: Be devoted and go deep—then deeper—in everything.

Self discipline, power: Do the things you know you have to do.

Order: Clean your life, but realize that nothing is perfect.

Stability, support: Find out what you need and ask for support.

Structure: Organize your life in a sustainable way.

Performance: Finish your tasks even if it is hard, rest in the things you know you have to do.

Afterword

Only tame birds have a longing. The wild ones fly.

ELMER DIKTONIUS

There have been many days when I have viewed the world with powerlessness, anger, and despair, but when wabi sabi entered my life, I started seeing the world with thoughtful eyes. The wisdom says that we all do the best we can with the things we are given. Nothing will ever be perfect, nor will it be finished or last forever.

The timeless wisdom teaches us to work together and move forwards in dance-like movements, where differences become our strength. Give and receive, treat yourself and the people around you with humor and warmth, and carefully walk where you need to go.

It may sound like a utopian idea to believe in peace and freedom on earth, but the wisdom, love, and kindness is actually the only thing that can create a good life and peace in the long run.

Beauty lives in the overflow created of kindness. The timeless wisdom informs us that there is nothing we can do or give to someone that will not come back to us full force. If I choose to attack someone with harsh words, I will soon be in the line of fire. Every smile I give another person creates a more smiling world.

Wabi sabi constantly takes us back to the fact that assessments, evaluations, and interpretations are meaningless. Tenderness, kindness, and a helping hand, on the other hand, create a good life. It is often hard to be human, and we have to accept our humanity and other people's humanity. None of us are perfect—but that's also where the beauty of life lies. When we see each other behind our masks and defenses, we will discover that we are all defenseless and vulnerable individuals that hungrily seek warmth, love, and community.

Wabi sabi can never promise that life will be solely easy, happy, or fun, but you can trust that you will feel great enjoyment when you give wabi sabi a place in your life.

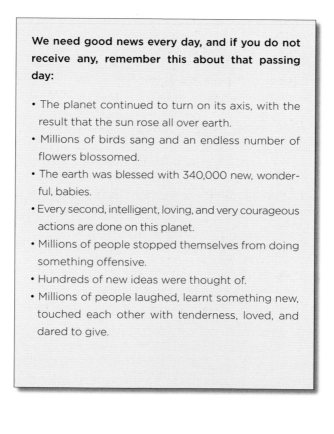

We need good news every day, and if you do not receive any, remember this about that passing day:

- The planet continued to turn on its axis, with the result that the sun rose all over earth.
- Millions of birds sang and an endless number of flowers blossomed.
- The earth was blessed with 340,000 new, wonderful, babies.
- Every second, intelligent, loving, and very courageous actions are done on this planet.
- Millions of people stopped themselves from doing something offensive.
- Hundreds of new ideas were thought of.
- Millions of people laughed, learnt something new, touched each other with tenderness, loved, and dared to give.

A NEW BEGINNING

Faithful Guide,
you sit at the gate of my life,
inviting me to eagerly enter
the newness stretching before me.
As I attend to the old burdens
that have weighted me down with worry,
I look ahead with hopeful expectation
to what my heart most needs.
I also recognize the absolute necessity
of living in the present moment.
I choose to direct my daily attentiveness
toward what will give my life greater balance.
I seek to let go of what keeps me unloving.
I long to contribute to peace in this world.

Often place the mirror of truth before me
so that I can see who I am
and how I need to go about my life.
Attune me daily to the beauty in all of creation.
Embrace me with your serenity and tender mercy.
I give you my love as I walk into this new beginning.

Once again, I place my confidence in you,
faithful companion and trusted guide.
You will show me the way to wholeness.

JOYCE RUPP, FROM *PRAYERS TO SOPHIA*

Reading tips

About wabi sabi
Simon Brown, *Practical Wabi Sabi*. Carroll and Brown Book Publishers, 2007.

Diane Durston, *Wabi Sabi*. Storey Publishing, 2006.

Taro Gold, *Living Wabi Sabi*. Andrews McMeel Publishing, 2004.

Andrew Juniper, *Wabi Sabi*. Tuttle Publishing, 2003.

Gregg Krech, *Naikan. Gratitude, Grace, and the Japanese Art of Self-Reflection*. Stone Bridge Press, 2002.

Richard R. Powell, *Wabi Sabi for Writers*. Adams Media, 2006.

Richard R. Powell, *Wabi Sabi Simple*. Adams Media, 2005.

Stories from a female perspective
Riane Eisler, *The chalice and the sword*. HarperOne, 1988.

Anita Goldman, *Våra bibliska mödrar*. Natur och kultur, 2010.

Birgitta Onsell, *Eer tusen år av tystnad. Gudinnebilder och glömda spår*. Carlsson, 2002.

Birgitta Onsell, *Galna gudar och glömda gudinnor*. LT, 1985.

Birgitta Onsell, *Jordens moder i Norden*. Carlsson, 1999.

Birgitta Onsell, *Morske män och menlösa mamseller*. En bok om roller och kön. LT, 1978.

Merlin Stone, *When God was a Woman*. Mariner Books, 1978.

Nature's wisdom, food, and environment
Cecilia Bertilsson och Mats Hellmark (red.), *Grön design*. Naturskyddsföreningen, 2008. Ingrid Franzon och Margareta Dahlberg, *Kanariefåglarna ryter. Din hälsa, vår miljö och en ljusnande framtid*. Örtagården, 2005.

Martin Gray, *Sacred* Earth. Sterling, 2007.

John Lane, *Timeless Beauty*. Green Books, 2004.

Mats-Eric Nilsson, *Den hemlige kocken. Det okända fusket med maten på din tallrik*. Ord-front, 2010.

Scott Olsen, *The Golden Section: Nature's Greatest Secret*. Walker and Company. 2006

Stephen Skinner, *Sacred Geometry*. Sterling, 2009.

Science

Gregg Braden, *The divine matrix*. Hay House. 2007.

Gregg Braden, *Övertygelsens kraft. Lär dig leva bortom falska begränsningar.* Ica, 2010.

Masaru Emoto, *The Hidden Messages in Water.* Beyond Words Pub Co. 2004.

Andrew Newberg, Eugene D'Aquili, Vince Rause, *Why God Won't Go Away.* Ballantine Books, 2002.

Life Knowledge

Sarah Ban Breathnach, *Inre rikedom – vägen till självkänsla, glädje och harmoni.* Forum, 1997.

Sarah Ban Breathnach, *Romancing the Ordinary.* Simon & Schuster, 2007.

Fynn, *Herr Gud, det är Anna.* Verbum, 1983.

Jerry Gillies, *Moneylove.* M. Evans & Company, 1978.

Ester och Jerry Hicks, *Ask and It is Given.* Hay House, 2005.

Gitte Jørgensen, *Simple living – nya vägar till ett meningsfullt liv.* Prisma, 2007.

Elisabeth Kübler-Ross, Döden är livsviktig. *Om livet, döden och livet efter döden.* Natur och kultur, 2003.

Giséla Linde, Lev enklare. *Idéer för en hållbar livsstil.* Viva, 2008.

Agneta Nyholm Winqvist, *Feng shui för själen.* Prisma, 2004.

Candice O'Denver, *En enkel förändring gör livet lätt. Om medvetenhet, visdom och medkänsla.* Energica, 2008.

Marshall B Rosenberg, *Being Me, Loving You. A Practical Guide to Extraordinary Relationships.* PuddleDancer Press, 2005.

Marshall B Rosenberg, *Nonviolent Communication: A Language of Life.* PuddleDancer Press, 2003.

Joyce Rupp, *Prayers to Sophia. A Companion to "The Star in My Heart".* Ave Maria Press, 2000.

Joyce Rupp, *The Star in My Heart. Experiencing Sophia, Inner Wisdom.* Ave Maria Press, 2004.

Regena Th omashauer, *Mama Gena's School of Womanly Art.* Simon & Schuster, 2003.

Owe Wikström, *Långsamhetens lov – eller vådan av att åka moped genom Louvren.* Natur och kultur, 2010.

Owe Wikström, *Sonjas godhet – medkänsla i en självupptagen tid.* Natur och kultur, 2008.

The twelve steps

Alcoholics anonymous often work after the following twelve-step program:

- We admitted we were powerless over our addiction—that our lives had become unmanageable
- Came to believe that a Power greater than ourselves could restore us to sanity
- Made a decision to turn our will and our lives over to the care of God as we understood God
- Made a searching and fearless moral inventory of ourselves
- Admitted to God, to ourselves and to another human being the exact nature of our wrongs
- Were entirely ready to have God remove all these defects of character
- Humbly asked God to remove our shortcomings
- Made a list of all persons we had harmed, and became willing to make amends to them all
- Made direct amends to such people wherever possible, except when to do so would injure them or others
- Continued to take personal inventory and when we were wrong promptly admitted it
- Sought through prayer and meditation to improve our conscious contact with God as we understood God, praying only for knowledge of God's will for us and the power to carry that out
- Having had a spiritual awakening as the result of these steps, we tried to carry this message to other addicts, and to practice these principles in all our affairs

Contact

Sofiainstitutet
Nybrogatan 19
871 31 Härnösand
Tel/fax 0611/751 51
www. soainstitutet.se
info@soainstitutet.se
School of Graceful Living, www.gracefulliving.se.

Agneta Nyholm Winqvist is one of the founders of the Sofia Institute and is a hand-leader at the institute's leadership development. The community builds on all-consuming, spiritual, timeless principles. The community is not tied to religion or politics; it works for a sustainable world and aches for peace and consensus. Beauty, wisdom, and freedom is the basis of the life view. The Sofia Institute gets their power and inspiration from nature. The Sofia Institute hosts, among other things, leadership development, retreats, peace and peace of mind seminars, child and youth activities women's circles, lighten-your-heart conversation, and alternative ordinances and ceremonies. The language of peace and the twelve-step program are the cornerstones of the community's activities. Agneta also has an interior design school called School of Graceful Living that blends feng shui, wabi sabi, timeless beauty, personal growth and health with green design, biomimicry, and sustainability.

Mira Malin Skogsdotter and Susanna Nova have taken most of the photos in this book. They work through the Temple of Spirited Living, a business where the basis is love for earth and the good in the human soul. They create touching beauty in their work with jewelry, ceremonial events, healing, decorating, photography, and raw food. They are a good example of women who have gone their own way to find existential answers.